JOURNEYS

Practice Book
Volume 1

Grade 3

HOUGHTON MIFFLIN HARCOURT
School Publishers

Credits

Illustrations: © Houghton Mifflin Harcourt Publishing Company

ISBN 10:   0-54-724638-2
ISBN 13:   978-0-54-724638-3

12   0928   15 14 13
4500412468

Contents

Contents

Words with Short Vowels

Read each word. Then find it in the Word Find.
Words can go across or down.

gentle	empty	visit	lily
softly	glance	puppy	tumble

```
s o v t l y u s o
p v i s i t s o y
u i l o g u f f s
p s y f e m p t y
p g l a n c e l t
y l i e t u m y o
p u l m l i l e s
t u y p e m y l y
b m u t u m b l e
```

Write each word in the correct place in the chart below.

Words with Short Vowels

a	e	i	o	u

The Subject of a Sentence

- A sentence is a group of words that tells a complete thought. The **subject** is the part of a sentence that tells whom or what the sentence is about.
- The subject usually comes at the beginning of the sentence. The subject can be one word or more than one word. The **complete subject** includes all the words in the subject.

  The weekend is a special time.
  My family enjoys their holidays.

Thinking Question
What word or words in the sentence tell whom or what the sentence is about?

Write the subject of each sentence.

1. Saturday is a fun day. _____

2. All my friends get together in the park. _____

3. Baseball teams play on the fields. _____

4. My father coaches the teams. _____

5. My mother watches all the games. _____

6. Our neighbors bring lots of food. _____

7. We cook outside until it is dark. _____

8. The kids sleep on a blanket. _____

9. Grandma and Grandpa tell stories. _____

10. Many of our teachers join us. _____

The Predicate of a Sentence

- Every sentence has two parts. The subject is one part of a sentence. The other part of the sentence is the predicate.
- The **predicate** is the part of a sentence that tells what the subject does or is.
- The predicate can be one word or more than one word. The **complete predicate** includes all the words in the predicate.

    I <u>lie beside the river.</u>

    My body <u>relaxes in the sun.</u>

Thinking Question
Which word or words in the sentence tell what the subject does or is?

Write each sentence. Then underline the predicate.

1. Relaxing is not as easy as it looks.

_____

2. I like to watch the clouds above me.

_____

3. Gerry enjoys floating in the pool.

_____

4. Ernie sits on the back steps with his dog.

_____

5. My cousins swing in tires hung from ropes.

_____

Story Structure

Read the selection below.

It was the first day of third grade. Emma walked to the front door to check the class lists. Mr. Hill was the teacher everyone wanted. Emma read his list first. All of her best friends' names were on the list, but not her own.

Next, she read Mrs. Smith's list. No one wanted to be in her room.

"Oh no!" Emma thought. "Not Mrs. Smith! I heard that she's mean!"

Emma walked down the third grade hallway. She was filled with dread. When she heard someone say, "Hi Emma! I'm glad you're here," she jerked her head up. It was Mrs. Smith!

Mrs. Smith shook Emma's hand and gave her a sweet smile. "We're going to have a great year!" she said.

Emma relaxed. It was hard to ignore Mrs. Smith's excitement. She decided it might be a good year after all.

Complete the Story Map to show the story structure.

Characters	Setting

Plot
Problem:
Events:
Solution:

Spelling Word Sort

A Fine, Fine School
Spelling:
Short Vowels

Write each Basic Word under the correct heading.
One word will go under two different headings.

Short *a*	Short *e*
_____	_____
_____	_____
_____	_____

Short *i*	Short *o*
_____	_____
_____	_____
_____	_____
_____	**Short *u***
_____	_____
_____	_____
_____	_____

Spelling Words

Basic
1. crop
2. plan
3. thing
4. smell
5. shut
6. sticky
7. spent
8. lunch
9. pumpkin
10. clock
11. gift
12. class
13. skip
14. swing

Review
next
hug

Challenge
hospital
fantastic

Review Add the Review Words to your Word Sort.

Challenge Which Challenge Word has short vowels *o* and *i*?

_____

Focus Trait: Word Choice
Exact Words

Without Exact Words	With Exact Words
Mr. Brown lived in a big house.	Mr. Brown lived in the enormous, old Victorian mansion on the hill behind Taft Middle School.

A. Read the sentence that does not use exact words. Then choose words and add details to make the description more exact.

Without Exact Words	With Exact Words
1. Every day I go to school.	Every _____ I _____ to _____.

B. Read each sentence that does not use exact words. Then look at the illustration on pages 26–27 of _A Fine, Fine School_. Rewrite the sentence using exact words.

Pair/Share Work with a partner to brainstorm exact words to use.

Without Exact Words	With Exact Words
2. The children are staying busy.	
3. Mr. Keene is making a face.	
4. The children are using their lockers.	

Words with the VCCV Pattern

Write a word from the box to complete each sentence in the story.

blossom	happened	suddenly
chipmunk	princess	garden
rabbit	puppet	trumpet
galloped		

1. The blaring _____ announced the show would soon begin.

2. Children sat in front of a little stage in the _____.

3. Everyone was excited to see the _____ show.

4. A furry _____ was the first puppet onstage.

5. Next came a little _____ puppet.

6. What _____ next was a surprise.

7. The rabbit told the chipmunk she was really a beautiful _____.

8. The chipmunk gave the rabbit a flower _____.

9. The rabbit _____ disappeared, and a beautiful princess stood in her place.

10. The princess and the chipmunk _____ away on a horse.

Story Structure

Read the selection below.

Samantha looked at her mother in disbelief. "What do you mean we have to go to school all year long?"

Samantha's mother read the newspaper article aloud. When Samantha stared at her with a confused look, she explained the school board's decision. "You will go to school from January through December," she said. "But you will still have three months off. They just won't all be in the summer."

"When will we go to Grandma's?" Samantha asked. "We always go in June and stay for two weeks."

"You'll still go in June and you'll still stay two weeks."

"What about winter break? We always have two weeks off for winter break," whined Samantha.

"Yes, you will still have two weeks off for winter break. You have two weeks off in March, two weeks off in June, four weeks off in August, two weeks in November, and two weeks in December."

"That sounds good!" Samantha said. "I never thought I'd say this," said Samantha, "but I want to go to school all year long!"

Use a Story Map to write information about the selection.
Then write your answers to the questions below.

1. How does Samantha first react when her mother says she will go to school all year long? Why does she act this way?

_____

2. How does Samantha's mother change Samantha's mind about year-round school?

_____

Complete Subjects and Predicates

Write the subject of each sentence.

1. Ira loves to read books in summer. _____

2. Gina enjoys sailing all summer. _____

3. Michaela rides her bike. _____

4. Wanda and Jane planted a garden. _____

5. The kids on Roy's block play baseball. _____

Write the predicate of each sentence.

6. Tera and her swim team travel on buses.

_____

7. The golf team has games all summer.

_____

8. Our dog sleeps most of the summer.

_____

9. Junie visits her grandparents.

_____

10. Cara builds houses for people.

_____

Name _____ Date _____

Short Vowels

Write a Basic Word to finish the second sentence in each pair of sentences.

1. Water is wet.

   Glue is _____.

2. You eat breakfast in the morning.

   You eat _____ at noon.

3. You use a ruler to measure length.

   You use a _____ to measure time.

4. Eyes help you see.

   A nose helps you _____.

5. A writer writes a book.

   A farmer plants a _____.

6. You can earn money by doing a job.

   When your money is gone, it is _____.

7. Watermelons are seen in summer.

   _____ are seen in fall.

8. A wolf belongs to a pack.

   A student belongs to a _____.

9. A horse learns to prance.

   A child learns to _____.

10. A key helps you open a door.

    When you leave, you _____ the door.

Challenge 11–12. Make up a pair of sentences similar to the ones above. Use a Challenge Word as the answer.

Spelling Words

Basic
1. crop
2. plan
3. thing
4. smell
5. shut
6. sticky
7. spent
8. lunch
9. pumpkin
10. clock
11. gift
12. class
13. skip
14. swing

Review
next
hug

Challenge
hospital
fantastic

Name _____ Date _____

Multiple-Meaning Words

Read the sentence. Write the meaning of the underlined word as it is used in the sentence. Think of another meaning for the underlined word. Use a dictionary if you need help. Write a sentence that includes that word and meaning.

1. One <u>fine</u> day when the sun was out, our family went on a picnic.

   _____

   _____

2. We ate sandwiches and tried a new <u>kind</u> of juice drink.

   _____

   _____

3. We got to <u>watch</u> people flying kites.

   _____

   _____

4. We rode a little <u>train</u> around the park.

   _____

   _____

5. We plan to take another <u>trip</u> to the park soon.

   _____

   _____

Name _____ Date _____

Writing Proper Nouns

- Nouns that name a day of the week, a holiday, a month of the year, a person's name, a person's title, or a book's title are called **proper nouns**.

  On a <u>Wednesday</u> in <u>November</u>, <u>Ms.</u> <u>Rodgers</u> had a <u>Thanksgiving</u> party.

  She read from her book, <u>Why Summer School?</u>

Identify the proper nouns in each sentence. Then write each sentence correctly.

1. Our school principal visited on mother's day.

_____

2. Our teacher will give a test next monday.

_____

3. The math teacher, ms. Davis, surprised all of us.

_____

4. One of my favorite books is <u>winter games</u>.

_____

5. In the U.S., july 4th is independence day.

_____

6. Did you see mr. clarke on sunday?

_____

Name _____ Date _____

Proofreading for Spelling

Read the following invitation. Find and circle the misspelled words.

You're Invited!

Please plen to attend Mr. Hay's cless next Monday.

We have spint three weeks learning about autumn. We want to share some of the thangs we learned with you.

We will begin when the cluck strikes ten. We will shet the doors at that time. We will teach you about some crups farmers grow in our area in the fall. Then we will discuss interesting facts about the sun and Earth at this time of year. Finally, we will eat. You will be hungry from the delicious smill of pompken pie! It will be our gaft to you.

Spelling Words

Basic
1. crop
2. plan
3. thing
4. smell
5. shut
6. sticky
7. spent
8. lunch
9. pumpkin
10. clock
11. gift
12. class
13. skip
14. swing

Review
next
hug

Challenge
hospital
fantastic

Write the misspelled words correctly on the lines below.

1. _____   6. _____

2. _____   7. _____

3. _____   8. _____

4. _____   9. _____

5. _____   10. _____

Sentence Fluency

Sometimes two sentences have the same predicate.
You can put the sentences together by combining the
subjects. The new sentence has more than one subject,
called a **compound subject**. This will make your
writing smoother.

Two Short Sentences with the Same Predicate	Smoother Sentences with a Compound Subject
Raul taught our cat to fetch. Winston taught our cat to fetch.	Raul and Winston taught our cat to fetch.
My sister showed the puppy tricks. My father showed the puppy tricks.	My sister and my father showed the puppy tricks.

**Combine two short sentences into one smoother sentence with a
compound subject. Write the sentence on the line.**

1. Our dog loves bones. Our cat loves bones.

   _____

2. Grandpa taught him a trick. Grandma taught him a trick.

   _____

3. Dogs love attention. Children love attention.

   _____

4. Danny taught our dog to sit. Alma taught our dog to sit.

   _____

5. The dog begged us to come. The cat begged us to come.

   _____

Words with Long Vowels

Read each clue. Write two rhyming words from the Word Bank to answer the clue.

base	rage	globe	joke
home	shade	skate	lime
broke	chase	plate	tone
probe	chrome	slime	phone
cage	shake	snake	trade

1. If you chase your friend around the bases on a field, you

play a game of _____ _____

2. If a joke wasn't funny, the _____ _____.

3. If a lime rots, you will have _____.

4. A snake that is cold does a dance called a _____

_____

5. An angry bird in a cage may get _____ _____

6. If you put paper plates under your feet, you can go for a _____

_____.

7. If you look up places on a globe, you play a game called

_____ _____.

8. If you switch shady spots, you do a _____ _____.

9. When you pick up a telephone, you hear a sound called a

_____ _____.

10. A shiny, silver house is a _____ _____

Statements and Questions

- Every sentence begins with a capital letter. There are four kinds of sentences. Statements and questions are two kinds.

- A sentence that tells something is a **statement**. It ends with a period. It is also called a **declarative** sentence.

- A sentence that asks something is a question. It ends with a question mark. It is also called an **interrogative** sentence.

   Statement/Declarative
   I wear comfortable clothes.

   Question/Interrogative
   What do you like to wear?

Thinking Question
Is the sentence a statement or a question, and what punctuation does it end with?

Write *statement* if the sentence tells something. Write *question* if the sentence asks something.

1. I wear old shirts around the house. _____

2. Why don't you go and change your clothes? _____

3. Who is coming to visit? _____

4. I dress up for company. _____

5. Why do my old clothes feel so good? _____

6. Old cotton shirts are very soft. _____

7. A new dress can feel strange. _____

8. My pet moves around the house. _____

Conclusions

Read the passage. Then complete the Inference Map.

Sam and Christy sat on a bench in the back yard. They stared unhappily at the garden tools and gloves their Mom had set out for them. Their sad faces suggested that this was not how they liked to spend Saturday morning. They started trying to think of an easier way to earn money.

"We could sell lemonade," said Christy.

"Nah," said Sam. "Last time we did that we only made four dollars. It would take forever to make enough money that way."

"How about walking dogs or putting on a talent show?" said Christy.

"We'd never be able to raise forty dollars walking dogs. And what talent do we have that people would pay to see?" asked Sam.

Christy sighed. "You're right. No one would pay to see us."

"We might as well face it," said Sam. "We're stuck weeding Mom's gardens for the next three Saturday mornings."

Christy groaned. "Mom sure knows how to make us remember the rules. I just hate weeding." She looked at the broken window next to the back door. "I'm *never* going to play baseball in the back yard again!"

Detail	Detail	Detail

Conclusion

Commands and Exclamations

- Two kinds of sentences are statements and questions. Two other kinds of sentences are **commands** and **exclamations**.

- A command is a sentence that tells someone to do something. It ends with a period. It is also called an **imperative** sentence.

- An exclamation is a sentence that shows strong feeling, such as excitement, surprise, or fear. It ends with an exclamation point. It is also called an **exclamatory** sentence.

- All kinds of sentences should begin with a capital letter and end with proper punctuation.

Thinking Question
Is the sentence a command or an exclamation, and what punctuation does it end with?

Command/Imperative	Get a chair, please.
Exclamation/Exclamatory	I'm excited!

**Write *command* if the sentence tells someone to do something.
Write *exclamation* if the sentence shows strong feeling.**

1. That is the funniest joke! _____

2. Tell another joke. _____

3. I am so happy! _____

4. Bring everyone in to hear these. _____

5. How my sides hurt from laughing! _____

6. Pull out those chairs and sit down. _____

7. Please repeat that joke. _____

Spelling Word Sort

Write each Basic Word under the correct heading.

Long *a*	Long *i*
1. _____	4. _____
2. _____	5. _____
3. _____	6. _____
	7. _____
	8. _____

Long *o*	Long *u*
9. _____	12. _____
10. _____	13. _____
11. _____	14. _____

Spelling Words

Basic
1. spoke
2. mile
3. save
4. excuse
5. cone
6. invite
7. cube
8. price
9. erase
10. ripe
11. broke
12. flame
13. life
14. rule

Review
these
those

Challenge
surprise
decide

Review What long vowel sound does the Review Word *these*

have? _____ What long vowel sound does the

Review Word *those* have? _____

Challenge In which column do the two Challenge Words

belong? _____

Focus Trait: Ideas
Audience and Purpose

Without Interesting Details	With Interesting Details
The milkman told the judge what he saw.	The milkman was sure the moose was guilty. He said Cardigan went up to the window and put his face close to the pie.

A. Read the sentence below. Rewrite the sentence with more interesting details to entertain your audience.

Without Interesting Details	With Interesting Details
1. The moose was clumsy.	

B. Read each sentence below. Rewrite the sentences, adding details that will make each one more interesting to the reader.

Pair/Share Work with a partner to find details to add to the sentences.

Without Interesting Details	With Interesting Details
2. Page 50: Mrs. Brown didn't know what happened to her pie.	
3. Page 62: The judge found the missing pie.	

Words with the VC*e* Pattern

**Read each word. Draw a line to match the word to
its meaning.**

Column 1

1. awake
2. costume
3. divide
4. escape
5. exercise
6. microphone
7. mistake
8. refuse
9. sidewalk
10. unite

Column 2

a. clothes worn to make somebody look like
somebody or something else
b. to free oneself or get away from
c. to bring things together
d. an error
e. not asleep
f. a paved path where people can walk
alongside a street
g. to separate
h. to say no
i. to work out or do a physical activity
j. a device to make someone's voice louder

**Write each word from Column 1 in the correct place in the
chart below. Look at the part of the word with the VC*e* pattern.**

Long *a*	Long *i*	Long *o*	Long *u*

Name _____ Date _____

Lesson 2
PRACTICE BOOK

The Trial of
Cardigan Jones
Deepen Comprehension:
Conclusions

Conclusions

Read the story below.

The Turner family drove out into the country for a picnic. After they finished their sandwiches, Keisha said, "Hurry and finish your Cheese Puffs, James, so we can go exploring." Her big brother was a slow eater.

"I'll finish them later," said James, putting the bag on top of the ice chest. He wiped the salty, orange powder off his fingers. "Let's go!"

The Turners sat on the blanket while four-year-old Ray-Ray played.

When James and Keisha came back, the Cheese Puffs bag was on the ground—empty!

"I think a bear ate them," said Keisha. She had been studying bears at school and knew that they would take human food from campsites.

"There are no bears around here," laughed James. "But there are a lot of raccoons. They use their paws just like little hands."

Just then Mrs. Turner noticed that Ray-Ray's shirt and hands were covered in orange grime. "I don't know how you get so dirty, Ray-Ray," she said, as she wiped his fingers clean.

Use an Inference Map to help you draw a conclusion about what happened. Then answer the questions.

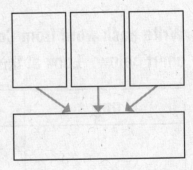

1. What conclusion did Keisha draw about the Cheese Puffs? Did you agree with her conclusion? Why or why not?

   _____

   _____

2. What conclusion did James draw about the Cheese Puffs? Did you agree with his conclusion? Why or why not?

   _____

   _____

Lesson 2
PRACTICE BOOK

**The Trial of
Cardigan Jones**
Grammar:
Kinds of Sentences

Statements, Questions, Commands, and Exclamations

Write *statement* if the sentence tells something. Write *question* if the sentence asks something.

1. I like basketball. _____

2. I would not want to climb a mountain. _____

3. Where do you row your boat? _____

4. Do you like to play tennis? _____

5. What do you know about judo? _____

Write *command* if the sentence tells someone to do something.
Write *exclamation* if the sentence shows strong feeling.

6. Pick up the tennis racket. _____

7. Tennis is a great sport! _____

8. Please join me in a game. _____

9. Ask him to play tennis with us. _____

10. I will not ask him! _____

Grammar
23
Grade 3, Unit 1: Good Citizens

V-C-*e* Spellings

Write the Basic Word that belongs in each group.

1. sphere, box, _____, _____

2. fire, smoke, _____

3. inch, yard, _____

4. ask, call, _____

5. ready, full-grown, _____

6. whispered, yelled, _____

7. law, principle, _____

8. change, wipe away, _____

9. rescue, free, _____

10. amount, cost, _____

Challenge Which Challenge Word belongs in a group called

Things That Are Unexpected? _____

Spelling Words

Basic
1. spoke
2. mile
3. save
4. excuse
5. cone
6. invite
7. cube
8. price
9. erase
10. ripe
11. broke
12. flame
13. life
14. rule

Review
these
those

Challenge
surprise
decide

Name _____ Date _____

Lesson 2
PRACTICE BOOK

**The Trial of
Cardigan Jones**
Vocabulary Strategies:
Compound Words

Compound Words

Read the compound words. On the first line, write the
two shorter words that make up the compound word. On the
second line, write a sentence using the compound word.

1. lunchbox

_____

_____

2. notebook

_____

_____

3. playground

_____

_____

4. classroom

_____

_____

5. homework

_____

_____

6. troublemaker

_____

_____

Name _____ Date _____

Using *a* and *an*, Adjectives with *-er* and *-est*

- The words *a* and *an* are special adjectives called **articles**. Use *a* and *an* with singular nouns. Use *a* before words that begin with a consonant sound. Use *an* before words that begin with a vowel sound.

- Add *-er* to most adjectives to compare two persons, places, or things. Add *-est* to most adjectives to compare *more than two* persons, places, or things.

    The dance will have <u>a</u> ticket charge, <u>an</u> invited band, and the <u>softest</u> music.

1–4. Write the correct word to finish each sentence.

1. I dance _____ (fast, faster) than her.

2. Ours is the _____ (prettier, prettiest) room of all.

3. The light is _____ (brighter, brightest) than the one in back.

4. Your cousin is the _____ (friendlier, friendliest) person I know.

5–8. Use proofreading marks to write each article or comparison in this letter correctly.

Dear Uncle Arnold,

I went to my first dance last night. I stayed out latest than I ever had before. There were all kinds of food and my favorite, a apple pie. We all danced in our finer clothes. The parents came. The teachers came, too. I was the happier boy in the world!

Love,
Gordon

Lesson 2
PRACTICE BOOK

The Trial of
Cardigan Jones
Spelling:
V-C-*e* Spellings

Proofreading for Spelling

Read the following invitation. Find and circle the misspelled words.

Do you sometimes wish there was no such thing as a roole? Let's think about how lief would be different without rules. You may surpris yourself and be thankful for rules!

Let's say you have an ice cream con. I see it and decid I want it. I take your ice cream. I do not say excoose me. I eat it all, even though you paid the prise for it.

Thos actions would make you mad, wouldn't they? But since there are no rules, the only thing I brok was your pride. I did not break a rule.

Rules saav us from situations like these. Rules help us all get along.

Write the misspelled words correctly on the lines below.

1. _____   6. _____

2. _____   7. _____

3. _____   8. _____

4. _____   9. _____

5. _____   10. _____

Spelling Words

Basic
1. spoke
2. mile
3. save
4. excuse
5. cone
6. invite
7. cube
8. price
9. erase
10. ripe
11. broke
12. flame
13. life
14. rule

Review
these
those

Challenge
surprise
decide

Lesson 2
PRACTICE BOOK

**The Trial of
Cardigan Jones**
Grammar:
Connect to Writing

Sentence Fluency

Sentences can be statements, questions, commands, or exclamations. Using all four kinds of sentences in a paragraph makes writing more lively and varied.

Paragraph with One Kind of Sentence	Paragraph with Four Kinds of Sentences
Rowing a boat can be lots of fun. You should try it. You find a boat. You will laugh a lot.	Rowing a boat can be lots of fun. Why don't you try it? Find a boat. You will not stop laughing!

Change each sentence to another type of sentence. The word in parentheses tells you the type of sentence to write. Write the new sentence on the line.

1. We won the boat race. (exclamation)

_____

2. Do you row the boats there? (statement)

_____

3. Can we put this boat in the water? (command)

_____

4. We should watch the boat race. (question)

_____

5. Will you let me ride in the boat? (statement)

_____

Common Vowel Pairs
ai, ay, ee, ea

Write the word from the Word Bank that best completes each sentence.

always	easel	stain	steam
bait	greedy	players	sweeten
breeze	holiday	queen	trail
chain	layers	seasons	

1. Of all the _____, fall is my favorite.

2. When you boil water, the _____ you see is the water vapor.

3. There was no school yesterday because it was a _____.

4. The door is secured with a lock and strong _____.

5. I knew it was the _____ because of her crown.

6. The hikers walked along the marked _____.

7. The artist paints at his _____.

8. To be safe, I _____ look both ways at a stop sign.

9. I will use honey to _____ the iced tea.

10. The cake has three different _____.

11. The spilled juice left a _____ on the carpet.

12. On a hot day, a _____ is welcome.

13. Remember to take the _____ with you when you go fishing.

14. Four _____ can play the game at the same time.

15. If you do not share, people may think you are _____.

Name _____ Date _____

Is It a Sentence?

- A **sentence** is a group of words that tells a complete thought. It tells whom or what, and it tells what happens.

    The whole neighborhood stood in the street.

- A group of words that is not a sentence is called a **fragment**. Parts of a sentence are missing.

    The whole neighborhood. Stood in the street.

Thinking Question
Does the sentence tell whom or what, and does it tell what happens?

Write *sentence* if the group of words is a sentence. Write *not a sentence* if it is not a sentence.

1. Men handed out papers. _____

2. Carried signs and shouted. _____

3. A large group of people. _____

4. The bookstore made money. _____

5. Everyone was happy. _____

Tell what is missing from the fragments. Write *Whom or what is missing* or write *What happened is missing.*

6. Young students and older friends. _____

7. Blocked off the street. _____

8. Played music and danced. _____

9. Long lines of readers. _____

10. Listened to the speeches and thought hard. _____

Understanding Characters

Read the selection below.

After dinner, Mom showed Carlos something that had come in the mail. It was pictures of animals at a shelter. The shelter was asking for money to take care of the animals. "I want to help those animals," said Carlos. "I'm going to raise money for the shelter." Just then, Carlos's older brother, Philip, came into the kitchen. Carlos told Philip about his plan to help. "I want to help, too," Philip said.

The very next day, Carlos started. Everywhere he went, he showed people the pictures and collected money. After a month, Carlos had raised over $500. Mom drove Carlos and Philip to the shelter. Carlos gave the manager the money. "I helped, too," Philip said. Mom took a picture of Carlos, Philip, and the manager. She put it in the newspaper.

Later, Mom asked Carlos why he let Philip take some of the credit for raising the money. Carlos explained, "I just want to help the animals." Mom smiled from ear to ear and gave Carlos a huge hug. "You did help them," she said.

Complete the Column Chart to show your understanding of Carlos and Philip.

Details About the Character	My Experience	What I Think

Correcting Fragments

- A complete sentence tells whom or what, and it tells what happens. Your writing will be easier to understand if you use complete sentences.

    ***Whom* or *What* Is Missing:**

    Wrote a long letter.

    ***Whom* or *What* Added:**

    <u>Theo</u> wrote a long letter.

    ***What Happens* Is Missing:**

    Susan with her pen.

    ***What Happens* Added:**

    Susan <u>writes</u> with her pen.

Thinking Question
Is the part of the sentence missing whom *or* what, *or is it missing* what happens?

Write the group of words that will make a sentence. Choose one of the groups of words below the sentence.

1. Last night, Dora _____.
   (pink paper; called people)

2. _____ called their friends.
   (In long sentences; Mom and Dad)

3. Other friends _____.
   (made phone calls; who are good people)

4. _____ got money in the mail.
   (Surprising us; The family)

5. The post office worker _____.
   (a lot of mail; brought it to us)

Spelling Word Sort

Write each Basic Word under the correct heading.

Long *a* Spelled *ay*	Long *a* Spelled *ai*
_____	_____
_____	_____
_____	_____
_____	_____

Long *e* Spelled *ee*	Long *e* Spelled *ea*
_____	_____
_____	_____
_____	_____
_____	_____
_____	_____

Review Add the Review Words to your Word Sort.

Challenge Add the Challenge Words to your Word Sort.

Spelling Words

Basic
1. lay
2. real
3. trail
4. sweet
5. today
6. dream
7. seem
8. tea
9. treat
10. afraid
11. leave
12. bait
13. screen
14. speed

Review
paint
please

Challenge
yesterday
explain

Focus Trait: Voice
Express Thoughts and Feelings

These thoughts and feelings…	…help you understand this.
Destiny remembers how much she enjoyed talking with writers. She describes how they shared her love of words.	They show how Destiny feels about talking to authors, and they explain why Destiny wanted to become a writer.

A. Read the event from *Destiny's Gift*. Underline the words that show Destiny's thoughts and feelings. Then explain what they help you understand about Destiny.

These thoughts and feelings…	…help you understand this.
1. Destiny can't stop crying after she finds out about Mrs. Wade's store.	

B. Read each sentence that tells an event from *Destiny's Gift*. Look at the page listed. Write a sentence that tells about Destiny's or Mrs. Wade's thoughts and feelings.

Pair/Share Work with a partner before you write.

Event	Sentence with Thoughts and Feelings
2. Page 80: Destiny says she likes Mrs. Wade's bookstore.	
3. Page 96: Destiny writes something for Mrs. Wade.	

Name _____ Date _____

Cumulative Review

Read the grocery list. Write each item in the chart below.

Grocery List

artichokes	grapes	peaches
beans	lemonade	peanuts
beef	limes	pineapple
cheese	grains	prunes
coffee	oatmeal	crayfish

	Long a		Long e	Long i spelled VC*e*	Long o spelled VC*e*	Long u spelled VC*e*
VC*e*		VC*e*				
ai		ee				
ay		ea				

Write a recipe on another sheet of paper. Use at least three words on the list. You can use other ingredients, too.

Name _____ Date _____

Understanding Characters

Read the selection below.

Dillon is ten years old. His little brother, Tate, is four. When Tate asks, "Can I come with you, Dillon?" Dillon always answers, "No, Tate. You're a baby!" This makes Tate cry. "I'm not a baby!" he protests.

When Tate tries to do what Dillon does, he gets hurt or gets in the way. Dillon yells, "You're too young to do this, Tate!"

One day, Dillon and Tate were at the park. Dillon's friends arrived with a soccer ball. "Want to play?" they asked Dillon.

"Yes," Dillon answered.

"Me, too," said Tate.

"You're too young," said one of Dillon's friends.

"Yes, you're a baby," said another.

Suddenly the hair on the back of Dillon's neck rose. His brow furrowed. "Tate is NOT too young!" he yelled. "He is NOT a baby!"

Dillon turned to Tate. "Come on, Tate. Let's go play on the swings."

"Okay," said Tate as they walked away from Dillon's friends.

Answer the questions about a character's motives.

1. When does Dillon call Tate a baby? Why does he do this?

_____

_____

2. What happens when Dillon's friends call Tate a baby?
Why does Dillon have this reaction?

_____

_____

Correct Run-ons

Destiny's Gift
Grammar:
Sentence Fragments and Run-ons

Two or more sentences that run together are called run-on sentences. Use end marks and capital letters correctly to keep sentences from running together.

do you want to find out more about moose go to the library

Do you want to find out more about moose? Go to the library.

Do not use a comma to separate two sentences.

I don't have any moose books, I'll go to the library.

I don't have any moose books. I'll go to the library.

Thinking Question
What correct end marks and capital letters will keep two sentences from running together?

Correct each run-on sentence. Write it as two sentences.

1. *Moose* is the American name for the largest deer it is called *elk* in Europe.

   _____

   _____

2. The name comes from *mos* the word is from a Maine Indian language.

   _____

   _____

3. Moose live in forests, they are comfortable in the cold.

   _____

   _____

More Long *a* and Long *e* Spellings

Destiny's Gift
Spelling:
More Long *a* and Long *e* Spellings

Write a Basic Word to answer each clue. Then use letters in the word to answer the second clue. The letters may not be in the correct order.

1. what helps you catch fish __ __ __ __

   what you swing in baseball __ __ __

2. how fast you go __ __ __ __ __

   not shallow __ __ __ __

3. something you do when you sleep __ __ __ __ __

   what you do with a book __ __ __ __

4. candy has this taste __ __ __ __ __

   a direction on a map __ __ __ __

5. a reward for a dog __ __ __ __ __

   what you do with food __ __ __

6. to go away __ __ __ __ __

   the night before a holiday __ __ __ __

7. to look or appear to be true __ __ __ __

   your eyes help you do this __ __ __

8. something you might walk on in the woods __ __ __ __ __

   a rodent with a long tail __ __ __ __

Spelling Words

Basic
1. lay
2. real
3. trail
4. sweet
5. today
6. dream
7. seem
8. tea
9. treat
10. afraid
11. leave
12. bait
13. screen
14. speed

Review
paint
please

Challenge
yesterday
explain

Antonyms

| lower | all | left |
| catch | take | last |

**Read each word below. Write the antonym from the box above.
Then write a sentence using both words.**

1. nothing _____

_____

2. first _____

_____

3. raise _____

_____

4. right _____

_____

5. throw _____

_____

6. give _____

_____

Writing Quotations

- Show what someone says by putting **quotation marks** (" ") at the beginning and the end of the speaker's exact words.

    Mom asked, "Have you finished studying?"
- Place a comma after words like *said* or *asked*. Use a capital letter for the first word of the quotation and an end mark inside the quotation marks.

    Greg said, "He just finished."

1–3. Write each sentence correctly using quotation marks.

1. John said, Please bring your lunch to the picnic.

_____

2. Grandfather asked, will you bring mine, too?

_____

3. I said, I will make you something special.

_____

4–8. Use proofreading marks to correct this paragraph.

My friend Gertie and I offered to help our neighbor. Mrs. Ling said "Why, I'd love it if you would help me." I asked, "where do you want us to start?" Mrs. Ling asked, "Do you know how to do dishes"? Gertie said, "I do!" She started washing, and I asked, "are you living here alone?" She said, "Yes I live here by myself. I said, "From now on we will help you."

Lesson 3
PRACTICE BOOK

Proofreading for Spelling

Destiny's Gift
Spelling:
More Long *a* and Long *e* Spellings

Read each sign. Find and circle the misspelled words.

Spelling Words

1.

Plees do not feed
the bears.

5.

The zoo will close
todaiy at 4 PM.

Basic
1. lay
2. real
3. trail
4. sweet
5. today

2.

Spead Limit
55
Miles per Hour

6.

Leeve your
shoes outside.

6. dream
7. seem
8. tea
9. treat
10. afraid

3.

Stay on the traiyl.

7.

Stay out!
Wet paynt.

11. leave
12. bait
13. screen
14. speed

4.

Sweete tee $1.00
Peanuts $.50

8.

Do not be afrad
to try new things.

Review
paint
please

Challenge
yesterday
explain

Write the misspelled words correctly on the lines below.

1. _____   5. _____

2. _____   6. _____

3. _____   7. _____

4. _____   8. _____

Grade 3, Unit 1: Good Citizens

Sentence Fluency

Too many short sentences make writing sound choppy.
Sometimes you can combine two short sentences to make
one longer sentence. Use a comma (,) and the conjunction
and, *but*, or *or* to combine two sentences.

Short Sentences	Compound Sentence
Libby owns many books. She hasn't read them all.	Libby owns many books, but she hasn't read them all.

**Combine the short sentences into compound sentences.
Use a conjunction.**

1. Victoria came to our book party. She brought ten books.

_____

_____

2. We could have the party on Saturday. We could wait until
Sunday.

_____

_____

3. People could bring books. They could bring magazines.

_____

_____

4. The books David brought were very interesting. They
were hard to understand.

_____

_____

Long *o* Spelled *oa*, *ow*

Each word in the Word Bank is in the puzzle. Find and circle
each word in the puzzle.

arrow	floating	undertow
below	goal	upload
blown	slow	
coach	throwing	

```
p u p l o a d n u p
o b l o p r r f n b
b l o w n e u l d e
e o t h r t h o e c
l c o a c h s a r o
o p w r a r l t t h
w b i l b r o i o b
n c a r r o w n w o
l o p e n i n g b a
g t h r o w i n g c
```

On a separate sheet of paper, use each word in the Word Bank in
a sentence. Read your sentences aloud.

Naming People, Places, and Things

- A word that names a person, a place, or a thing is a **noun**.

    My <u>mom</u> helped to build the new <u>road</u>.
    The <u>work</u> lasted one <u>year</u>.

Thinking Question
Is the word naming a person, a place, or a thing?

Write the two nouns in each sentence.

1. Workers brought in tables. _____

2. High winds knocked down the tents. _____

3. The sand blew into the food. _____

4. The moon was beautiful at night. _____

5. My family did some work. _____

6. My cousin showed the workers where to go.

    _____

7. My brother played some music. _____

8. My uncle put up the signs. _____

9. Her mother brought food sometimes. _____

10. The mayor visited when the road was done.

    _____

Compare and Contrast

Read the selection below.

The boy selling newspapers yelled the headline, "Bridge Complete!" His stack of papers was disappearing quickly. Even Mom bought one. "What's the big deal?" Samuel asked her.

"The Golden Gate Bridge is finished!" she answered him. Samuel was curious but still not impressed. "It's just a bridge," he thought to himself.

That afternoon, Dad announced, "There's a parade at the bridge tomorrow. I want us to be there to celebrate!" The next day, Samuel left to go to the parade. He still didn't understand why everyone was making such a big deal out of the new bridge. He wanted to find out.

At the bridge, Samuel and his family joined the crowd and waited. Then, a foghorn sounded and everyone began walking across the bridge. Samuel looked up at the bridge. He looked down at the swirling tide. This bridge was a huge project. Its completion was a statement. It said America was strong, just like this bridge. Samuel was proud to be crossing the bridge with his family. Now Samuel wanted to know more about the bridge.

Complete the Venn diagram to show how Samuel changes and how he stays the same.

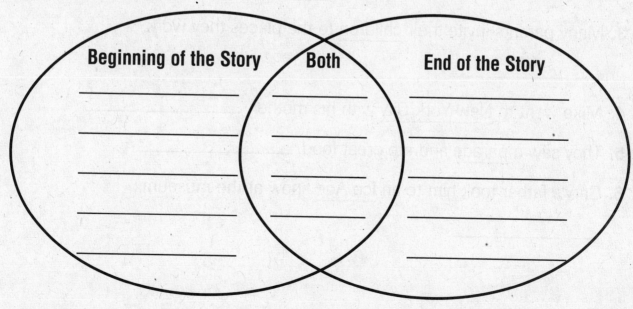

Beginning of the Story   Both   End of the Story

Grade 3, Unit 1: Good Citizens

Common and Proper Nouns

- A word that names a person, place, or thing is a noun.
- A noun that names any person, place, or thing is called a **common noun**. A noun that names a particular person, place, or thing is called a **proper noun**.
- Proper nouns begin with capital letters. A proper noun may have more than one word. Begin each important word in a proper noun with a capital letter.

    His daughter Audrey visited him at his job in England.

> **Thinking Question**
> *Does the noun name any person, place, or thing, or does it name a particular person, place, or thing?*

Write *common* or *proper* for each underlined noun.

1. Outside of Atlanta, Jessie's father works in an office. _____

2. Bennie came to his father's candy shop. _____

3. Many parents invite their children to the places they work.

    _____

4. Mike went to New York City with his mother. _____

5. They saw a parade and ate great food. _____

6. Gary's father took him to an Ice Age show at the museum.

    _____

Spelling Word Sort

Pop's Bridge
Spelling:
More Long *o* Spellings

Write each Basic Word under the correct heading.

Long *o* Spelled *o*	Long *o* Spelled *ow*
_____	_____
_____	_____
_____	_____
_____	_____
_____	_____

Long *o* Spelled *oa*
_____
_____
_____
_____
_____
_____

Spelling Words

Basic
1. load
2. open
3. told
4. yellow
5. soak
6. shadow
7. foam
8. follow
9. glow
10. sold
11. window
12. coach
13. almost
14. throat

Review
cold
most

Challenge
tomorrow
sailboats

Review Add the Review Words to your Word Sort.

Challenge Add the Challenge Words to your Word Sort.

Grade 3, Unit 1: Good Citizens

Focus Trait: Ideas
Important and Interesting Details

Good writers use interesting details to help readers understand their ideas.

For example:

The girl rode her bike.

The above sentence would be much more interesting with important details added:

The small redheaded girl proudly rode her shiny new yellow bike to school.

Read each sentence and look at the illustration from "Pop's Bridge" on the page listed. Add interesting details to each sentence.

1. Page 122: The family looked at the bridge.

   _____

   _____

2. Page 125: The boy shouted on the street.

   _____

   _____

3. Page 131: Robert was happy.

   _____

   _____

4. Page 132: He cut the puzzle piece.

   _____

   _____

Cumulative Review

Read each clue. Unscramble the letters and write the word that answers the clue. Read the words you made.

1. This is a food. Many people eat it in the morning. mtoeala _____

2. You might do this if you do not want to do something. anlcopmi _____

3. Cars drive fast on these kinds of roads. They have two or more lanes. whgysiha _____

4. This is a way to heat bread. tasot _____

5. This can take you across the sea, when it's windy. alitabos _____

6. This number is the answer to these math problems: 5 X 3 and 5 + 5 + 5. efnietf _____

7. There are four of these. They are winter, spring, summer, and fall. eosnsas _____

8. This is the color of a lemon. lelwyo _____

9. This describes something that never moves very quickly. wols _____

10. This can help you find your way when you are driving. pdraaom _____

Compare and Contrast

Read the selection below.

Payton sat down with the book from school. He was not looking forward to this assignment. He enjoyed reading, but he liked to read mysteries and science fiction. This was historical fiction. Payton didn't enjoy history.

Sitting in his favorite chair, Payton read the first chapter. He must have read the first page ten times. He couldn't seem to understand the meaning of the words. But he kept on. There would be a quiz the next day on the first three chapters.

Chapter 2 captured Payton's attention. He actually enjoyed reading about the main character's life, even though the action was happening in 1930. Payton finished Chapter 3. He closed the book and stared at the cover. He thought of the familiar saying, "Never judge a book by its cover." This may not end up being one of Payton's favorite books, but he had to admit he thought he would enjoy it after all.

Compare and contrast Payton's experience with your own. Complete a Venn diagram like the one here and answer the questions below.

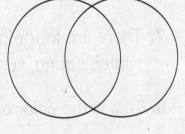

1. Describe an event from this story that reminds you of your own life. How are the events similar?

_____

_____

_____

2. Describe how you and the main character are different.

_____

_____

Common and Proper Nouns

1–5. Write the two nouns in each sentence.

1. The boys watched the hotel being taken down. _____

2. A large ball knocked down the old walls. _____

3. A new building would go up in that space. _____

4. Soon, a huge hole was in the ground. _____

5. In a few years, a skyscraper would be there. _____

6–10. Write *common* or *proper* for each underlined noun.

6. We learned about the Middle Ages in school. _____

7. My aunt came all the way from Canada. _____

8. The crowd rode horses. _____

9. It was an exciting day. _____

10. My friends live near the Brooklyn Bridge. _____

More Long *o* Spellings

In the spaces below, write a Spelling Word to complete each newspaper ad.

1.

The Shoe Store is _____! Come in and try on a pair of our great shoes.

4.

Do you like baseball? Baseball _____ needed to work with children. Apply in person.

2.

_____ Washers We'll clean your glass!

5.

Garage Sale today and _____. _____ the signs to our house.

3.

Enjoy the _____ of a warm fire! Buy a _____ of our firewood.

6.

Store Closing Sale We cannot close until everything is _____.

Spelling Words

Basic
1. load
2. open
3. told
4. yellow
5. soak
6. shadow
7. foam
8. follow
9. glow
10. sold
11. window
12. coach
13. almost
14. throat

Review
cold
most

Challenge
tomorrow
sailboats

1. _____

2. _____

3. _____ , _____

4. _____

5. _____ , _____

6. _____

Lesson 4
PRACTICE BOOK

Pop's Bridge
Vocabulary Strategies:
Base Words and Endings *-s, -es,*
-ed, -ing

Word Endings
-s, *-es*, *-ed*, *-ing*

disappear	remind	call
push	support	form
balance	construct	

**For each item, choose a base word from the list above. Add *-s*
or *-es*, *-ing,* and *-ed* to the base word. On each line, write a
sentence that shows the meaning of each form of the word.**

1. _____

_____

_____

2. _____

_____

_____

Correct Pronouns

- A **noun** names a person, a place, or a thing. The **pronouns** *I*, *he*, *she*, *it*, *we*, and *they* can take the place of a noun in the subject of a sentence.
- Use a pronoun that matches, or agrees with, the noun it replaces.
- When you write or talk about another person and yourself, name yourself last. *I* should always be a capital letter.

  Nina and **I** shared the umbrella.

1–4. Write the correct pronoun for the underlined pronoun.

1. Roy and <u>me</u> wear our helmets. _____

2. Len said <u>him</u> would bring his own gloves. _____

3. Jorge and <u>me</u> are very careful. _____

4. Morris and <u>me</u> wear seat belts. _____

5–8. Use proofreading marks to write each pronoun in this letter correctly.

Dear Mr. Kelvin,

I will bring my binoculars when us go to the park tomorrow. Is Jenny coming? Will her bring binoculars? Her brother can use mine if him wants.

Jenny and me enjoyed the last trip we took to the park.

Sincerely,

Paul Smith

Pop's Bridge
Spelling:
More Long *o* Spellings

Proofreading for Spelling

Read the following newspaper article. Find and circle the misspelled words.

Yelloaw Jackets Win First Game

The stadium was owpen for the game. Coch Smith and her players were ready. The game was sould out. Not even the coald weather kept people away. The crowd cheered as the team entered the stadium.

The first batter scored a run almowst right away. During the game, nine more players folloawed her lead. The Yellow Jackets left the other team in the shados.

A player towld me after the game that they intend to win every game this season. They will be put to the test tomorroaw when they play the Colts.

Spelling Words

Basic
1. load
2. open
3. told
4. yellow
5. soak
6. shadow
7. foam
8. follow
9. glow
10. sold
11. window
12. coach
13. almost
14. throat

Review
cold
most

Challenge
tomorrow
sailboats

Write the misspelled words correctly on the lines below.

1. _____   6. _____
2. _____   7. _____
3. _____   8. _____
4. _____   9. _____
5. _____   10. _____

Name _____ Date _____

Word Choice

Using **exact nouns** helps make your writing clearer and more interesting.

Less-Exact Noun	More-Exact Noun
road	superhighway
area	valley

Replace each underlined noun in the sentences with a more exact noun. Use the nouns in the word box.

ranch	coyotes	ponies
thunderstorms	city	cowboys

1. Ernie saw two <u>men</u> through his binoculars. _____

2. They were rounding up some <u>animals</u>. _____

3. Off to one side, some <u>wild animals</u> were hard to see. _____

4. Faraway, the sky was filled with <u>rain</u>. _____

5. They worked hard to get people back to their <u>home</u>. _____

Name _____ Date _____

Long *i* Spelled *i, ie, igh*

Roberto Clemente, Pride of the Pittsburgh Pirates
Phonics:
Long *i* Spelled *i, ie, igh*

Read each sentence. Choose the missing word from the box. Write the word in the blank.

find	climb	fried
sights	wild	lie
sigh	untied	
tried	midnight	

1. I did not _____ the book I was looking for.

2. The clock strikes twelve at _____.

3. Jasmine and her family went to Paris to see the

_____.

4. The _____ animal ran through the forest.

5. I would like to _____ a mountain some day.

6. I tripped over my shoelaces because they were

_____.

7. The best dish at this restaurant is _____ chicken.

8. "I wish it would stop raining," Marty said with a

_____.

9. The police officer _____ to direct traffic.

10. George Washington once said, "I cannot tell a

_____."

Lesson 5
PRACTICE BOOK

**Roberto Clemente, Pride
of the Pittsburgh Pirates**
Grammar:
Plural Nouns with -s and -es

Plural Nouns with -s

- A noun that names only one person, place, or thing is a **singular noun**. A noun that names more than one person, place, or thing is a **plural noun**.
- Add -s to most singular nouns to form the plural.

> The Egyptians played a ball <u>game</u>.
> The Egyptians played ball <u>games</u>.
> They ran from place to <u>place</u>.
> They ran to different <u>places</u>.

Thinking Question
Is the word naming only one person, place, or thing or more than one person, place, or thing?

1–4. Write singular or plural for each underlined noun.

1. Many <u>kids</u> played ball games long ago. _____

2. The <u>ball</u> was made of cloth. _____

3. One player ran between two <u>stones</u>. _____

4. They would throw the ball at a <u>runner</u>. _____

5–8. Write the plural form of the noun in parentheses to complete the sentence.

5. Later, teams drew _____ on the field. (line)

6. Teams built _____ for another edge of the field. (wall)

7. Some _____ would throw the ball underhand. (pitcher)

8. Some games would last twelve _____. (hour)

Cause and Effect

Read the selection below.

The 1920s were a long time ago, but Babe Ruth is still remembered. Many people think that he was the greatest baseball player of all time.

He began his career with the Boston Red Sox as a pitcher. Soon however, his batting skill became the focus of attention. He was traded to the New York Yankees in 1920, and his career as a home-run hitter took off. He hit 54 home runs that year. In 1927, he hit 60. That record lasted until 1961.

Perhaps his most famous moment came during the third game of the 1932 World Series against the Chicago Cubs. However, no one knows whether that moment ever really happened! Legend says that when Cub fans were yelling at Ruth, he pointed to center field. He hit the next pitch to the very place he'd pointed to. The ball sailed over the center field wall for a towering home run! Whether true or not, it's a great story.

Complete the T-Map to show causes and effects from the selection.

Cause	Effect

Plural Nouns with *-s*

**Roberto Clemente, Pride
of the Pittsburgh Pirates**
Grammar:
Plural Nouns with *-s* and *-es*

> • Add *-s* to most nouns to form the plural.
>
> **Singular:**   *team*   *cap*   *bat*
> **Plural:**   *teams*   *caps*   *bats*

Thinking Question
*Do I add -s to form
the plural?*

Write the plural form of the underlined noun.

1. They put a new <u>stain</u> on the floor.

They tested two different _____ to see which would be
darker.

2. Portia slipped and fell with a loud <u>bang</u>.

A few minutes later, there were two louder _____.

3. The basketball <u>player</u> wore high-top sneakers.

More _____ started wearing them after the first game.

4. The <u>light</u> came on when he fell into the switch.

After three people fell, more _____ came on.

5. They put a <u>sign</u> on the ground to warn people not to slip.

At the end of the day, there were a dozen _____ in that area.

Spelling Word Sort

Roberto Clemente, Pride
of the Pittsburgh Pirates
Spelling:
Spelling Long *i*

Write each Basic Word under the correct heading.

Long *i* Spelled *i*	Long *i* Spelled *ie*
_____	_____
_____	_____
_____	_____
_____	_____
_____	

Long *i* Spelled *igh*	
_____	_____
_____	_____
_____	_____

Review   Add the Review Words to your Word Sort.

Challenge   What letter or letters form the long *i* sound in the two Challenge Words?

_____ ; _____

Spelling Words

Basic
1. slight
2. mild
3. sight
4. pie
5. mind
6. tie
7. pilot
8. might
9. lie
10. tight
11. blind
12. fight
13. die
14. midnight

Review
find
night

Challenge
silent
frightening

Name _____ Date _____

Lesson 5
PRACTICE BOOK

Roberto Clemente, Pride
of the Pittsburgh Pirates
Writing:
Write to Narrate

Focus Trait: Sentence Fluency
Time-Order Words

Writers use transition words, or time-order words, to show
when events happen. For example:

After they won the championship game, all the boys on
Pedro's soccer team cheered and high-fived each other.
Next, they went out for pizza to celebrate.

**Read the following paragraph. In each blank, fill in the most
logical phrase from the box.**

Then	Yesterday morning
Afterwards	During the game
Before I left the house	When I got to the field

1. _____, I woke up with butterflies in
my stomach. It was the day of my first softball game!
Immediately, I jumped out of bed. 2. _____,
I put on my new uniform and ran downstairs
for breakfast. 3. _____, I
reminded my mother to take the camera to the game.
4. _____, my teammates were
there practicing. 5. _____, I got two hits
and one run! In the end, we won the game by one
point. 6. _____, my mother took me out for
ice cream.

Cumulative Review

Write a word from the box to complete each sentence.

most	lightning	flowed
slimy	toast	railroad
tries	knights	
glowing	title	

1. Lava _____ down the sides of the volcano and into the sea.

2. A bolt of _____ suddenly flashed across the sky.

3. The _____ of my favorite book is *White Fang*.

4. For breakfast, Karl likes to eat _____ with peanut butter.

5. I love to watch the fireflies _____ in the dark summer sky.

6. King Arthur and his _____ sat at a huge round table.

7. The worm felt _____ when I touched it.

8. Always stop, look, and listen before crossing a _____ track.

9. The athlete finally jumped over the bar after three _____.

10. Lee knew _____ of the answers on the test, but not all
of them.

Cause and Effect

Read the selection below.

Tiger Woods, born in 1975, is one of the most successful and talented golfers of all time. His father, Earl Woods, nicknamed him "Tiger" after a Vietnamese soldier who saved Earl's life during the Vietnam War. Tiger's parents were a major influence in his life. His father taught him to believe in himself and work hard for his goals. His mother helped him become more patient. She never tired of driving him to tournament sites when he was still a child.

When Tiger was only eleven months old, he began swinging a miniature golf club in his parents' garage. At two, he showed his putting skill on a national TV show. That was just the beginning of Tiger's rise to fame. In 1997 he became the first African American to win the Masters Tournament. Tiger Woods has won more major golf tournaments than any other professional golfer playing today.

Use a T-Map to show causes and effects from the selection.
Then answer the questions.

Cause	Effect

1. Why did Earl Woods nickname his son "Tiger"?

_____

_____

2. Why do you think Tiger Woods has been so successful in life?

_____

_____

_____

Plural Nouns with *-s* and *-es*

Roberto Clemente, Pride
of the Pittsburgh Pirates
Grammar:
Plural Nouns with *-s* and *-es*

1–5. Write singular or plural for each underlined noun.

1. The fans went to find their <u>seats</u>. _____

2. The popcorn seller brought them two <u>boxes</u>.

   _____

3. Other fans passed a giant <u>ball</u> around.

   _____

4. A foul ball sailed up into the stands from the <u>field</u>.

   _____

5. Some fans had special <u>passes</u> that let them go onto the

   field. _____

**6–10. Write the plural form of the noun in parentheses to
complete the sentence.**

6. Two _____ had wire mesh that stopped foul
   balls. (fence)

7. People stood in the _____ instead of sitting
   in their seats. (aisle)

8. The fans clapped for a series of great _____
   of hard-hit balls. (catch)

9. The scoreboard could not show any _____,
   because that number was broken. (six)

10. There were _____ of programs to hand out
    to the fans. (stack)

Roberto Clemente, Pride of the Pittsburgh Pirates
Spelling:
Spelling Long *i*

Spelling Long *i*

Write a Basic Word to answer each question.

1. If you were eating a round dessert with a flaky crust, what would you be eating? _____

2. What is the opposite of loose? _____

3. What is the time when one day becomes another?

_____

4. What would a man wear around his neck if he was getting dressed up? _____

5. What is the opposite of a true statement?

_____

6. Who flies a plane? _____

7. What do you think with? _____

8. What does a boxer have to do? _____

Spelling Words

Basic
1. slight
2. mild
3. sight
4. pie
5. mind
6. tie
7. pilot
8. might
9. lie
10. tight
11. blind
12. fight
13. die
14. midnight

Review
find
night

Challenge
silent
frightening

Prefix *mis-*

Read the letter. Notice the underlined words. Write a reply to this letter. Use at least four of the underlined words in your letter.

Dear Friend,

    I did not mean to <u>misbehave</u> or <u>mistreat</u> you. I thought it was funny when someone <u>mispronounced</u> your name. I didn't think it would upset you, but I can see that I <u>miscalculated</u> that. If someone said I did not want to be your friend, then they are <u>misinformed</u>. Can we please forget about this <u>misunderstanding</u>?

Your friend

_____

_____

_____

_____

_____

_____

_____

_____

67

Lesson 5
PRACTICE BOOK

Roberto Clemente, Pride of the Pittsburgh Pirates
Grammar:
Spiral Review

Commas in Sentences

- **Commas** are used in a date or when listing city and state in a sentence.
- **Commas** are also used when combining sentences and when using nouns or verbs in a series.

  On June 3, 1973, in Chicago, Illinois, they played baseball, football, and soccer.

1–2. Rewrite each sentence with a comma where it belongs in a date or a place.

1. They loaded the plane bringing supplies on December 29 1972.

_____

2. It was headed for Managua Nicaragua.

_____

3–4. Combine each group of sentences. Put the nouns or verbs in a series with commas. Write the new sentence.

3. The plane carried food. The plane carried water. The plane carried supplies.

_____

4. A pilot was onboard. A baseball star was onboard. A helper was onboard.

_____

Proofreading for Spelling

Find the misspelled words and circle them.

Spelling Words

Basic
1. slight
2. mild
3. sight
4. pie
5. mind
6. tie
7. pilot
8. might
9. lie
10. tight
11. blind
12. fight
13. die
14. midnight

Review
find
night

Challenge
silent
frightening

Plane Has Narrow Escape

A brave pielot saved the lives of her passengers yesterday when she saved an airplane from crashing.

Captain Jo Ann Foster was flying at 35,000 feet at midnite when her plane began to rock. There was only a sliet wind, so she knew her plane was in trouble. An engine was out, and the plane was sinking. Not only that, but thick fog made her have to fly blighnd. She was in a tite spot.

Captain Foster quickly thought of things she mite do. Different ideas went through her miend. She would have to fite to guide her plane to safety.

"I felt some miled fear," she said later, "but I was mainly thinking of how to save the plane and the passengers."

She found the nearest airport on the map and steered toward it. Finally, the airport came in siet. Captain Foster made a perfect landing, and 147 passengers were safe.

Write the misspelled words correctly on the lines below.

1. _____   6. _____

2. _____   7. _____

3. _____   8. _____

4. _____   9. _____

5. _____   10. _____

Conventions: Proofreading

Using the correct spelling of plural nouns makes your writing clearer and easier to understand. Add *-s* to form the plural of most singular nouns. Add *-es* to form the plural of a singular noun that ends with *s, sh, ch,* or *x*.

Sentences With Singular Nouns That Should be Plural Nouns	Sentences with Correct Plural Nouns
The baseball player tried two bat before choosing one.	The baseball player tried two bats before choosing one.
The teams sat on two bench.	The team sat on two benches.

Circle the singular noun that should be plural in each sentence. Then write the sentence using the plural spelling of the noun.

1. The fans rode to the baseball game in ten bus.

   _____

2. Most of the fans have already been to some game this year.

   _____

3. Juan and Mary took their baseball glove to the game.

   _____

4. The pitcher made two great catch.

   _____

5. Another player made two good toss to first base.

   _____

VCV Words with Long and Short Vowels

Read each sentence. Choose the missing word from the box.
Write the word. Then reread the complete sentence.

visit	robot	flavor
tiny	limit	shiver
report	decide	gravel

1. We took a bumpy ride down a _____ road in the country.

2. Chocolate is my favorite _____.

3. I _____ the amount of sweets that I eat.

4. My sister has a collection of _____ glass animals.

5. I need to pick a topic for my _____.

6. It was hard to _____ which movie to watch.

7. The icy wind made me _____.

8. Steve hopes to _____ the Space Museum someday.

9. That interesting machine is called a _____.

Action Verbs

> A word that tells what people or things do is a **verb**.
> Words that show action are **action verbs**.
>
> > *Tyler **shines** his coins.*
> >
> > *Juana **purchased** stamps at the post office.*

Thinking Question
What is the subject doing?

Each sentence has one action verb. Write the action verb on the line.

1. My brother puts things in boxes. _____

2. He looked for glass on the beach. _____

3. His friend gave him old bottles. _____

4. My mother found toys. _____

5. My dad took some of his things. _____

6. Harry saw a beautiful picture. _____

7. He bought it from the shopkeeper. _____

8. Someone carried a sled to my brother. _____

9. He and his friend tied it to a tree. _____

10. Everyone came to the tree. _____

Name _____ Date _____

Sequence of Events

Read the selection below.

Mason was bored. His best friend Jorge was at summer camp.
Mason had just finished reading Jorge's letter. The letter said Jorge
collected a special badge for each fun activity he learned to do.
Mason sighed. He sure wasn't collecting any badges.

Suddenly, Mason's mood changed. "I can collect something!" he
thought. "I can hike the mountain trails near here. I'll collect things I find."

That afternoon, Mason and his older brother hiked Rainbow Trail. They
found interesting rocks and a stone arrowhead. When he got home, Mason
arranged his treasures in shoeboxes. Then he made labels.

After that, Mason hiked and collected every day. He set up the
collection on tables in the garage. Then he hung a sign on the garage door.

When Jorge came back, the first thing he noticed was Mason's sign. It
read "Mason's Mountain Museum."

**Use a Flow Chart to track the order of events in the selection.
Then use your Flow Chart to respond to the items below.**

1. What happened after Mason got a letter from Jorge?

_____

_____

_____

2. How did Mason's feelings change after he had started his
   collection?

_____

_____

_____

Name _____ Date _____

Lesson 6
PRACTICE BOOK

Max's Words
Grammar:
What Is a Verb?

Being Verbs

Some verbs do not show action. The verbs *am*, *is*, *are*, *was*, and *were* are forms of the verb *be*. They tell what someone or something is or was.

> I *am* interested in fine china.
> I *was* proud of my coin collection.
> They *are* the neatest stamp mounters.
> You *were* last at the post office.
> He *is* skilled at identifying coins.
> We *were* nervous at the exhibition.

Am, *is*, and *are* show present tense. *Was* and *were* show past tense.

Thinking Question
What is or was the subject?

Write the being verb on the line. Write *present* or *past* for each verb.

1. My father was nice to us. _____

2. He is kind and gives us his coins. _____

3. We were nice to him. _____

4. The boys are angry when they lose points. _____

5. You are good to help us. _____

6. Most people are open to the idea. _____

7. They were funny when we asked. _____

8. They are upset sometimes but not often. _____

9. I am careful to ask nicely. _____

10. I was friendly to everyone. _____

More Short and Long Vowels

Write each Basic Word in the box where it belongs. You will
write words with two vowel sounds in more than one box.

Vowel sound in *rope*	Vowel sound in *meet*
_____	_____
_____	_____
_____	_____
_____	

Vowel sound in *came*	Vowel sound in *bite*
_____	_____
_____	_____
_____	_____

Vowel sound in *blue*	Vowel sound in *flat*
_____	_____
_____	_____

Vowel sound in *cup*	Vowel sound in *dress*
_____	_____

Vowel sound in *skip*	Vowel sound in *odd*
_____	_____
_____	_____

Spelling Words

Basic
1. math
2. toast
3. easy
4. socks
5. Friday
6. stuff
7. paid
8. cheese
9. June
10. elbow
11. program
12. shiny
13. piles
14. sticky

Review
each
both

Challenge
comb
holiday

Challenge   Add the Challenge Words to your Word Sort.

Focus Trait: Ideas
Details and Examples

Writer's Idea	Details and Examples
Karl's coins are different from each other.	They came in different sizes and colors. The silver ones had rough edges. The copper ones had smooth edges.

A. Read each of the writer's ideas. Find the details and examples from *Max's Words* that help explain the idea. Complete the sentences.

Writer's Idea	Details and Examples
1. Max collects many words.	He _____ small words and bigger words out of _____ and _____.
2. Max organizes his words in a special way.	He took his words off his _____ and put them _____. Then he neatly arranged them into _____.

B. Read each of the writer's ideas. Look at the pages from *Max's Words*. Write details and examples that help explain each idea.

Pair/Share   Work with a partner to find details and examples in the story.

Writer's Idea	Details and Examples
3. It makes a big difference when Max arranges his words in different orders. (p. 202)	
4. Max tries to use his words to get what he wants. (p. 204)	

Cumulative Review

Write a word from the box to complete each sentence. Then read the complete sentence.

pilot	planet	tiger
second	visit	bacon
flavor	finish	cabins

1. Can we play outside after we _____ our homework?

2. My cousins came to _____ us last summer.

3. As we were leaving the plane, the _____ shook my hand.

4. The scouts stayed in small _____ near the lake.

5. Chocolate is the _____ of ice cream that I like best.

6. Do you want _____ with your eggs?

7. Look! That reddish light in the sky is the _____ Mars!

8. Brad came in _____ in the race, right behind Jay.

9. We watched a _____ sleep under the tree.

Sequence of Events

Read the selection below.

1   One day, Marisa's teacher asked that each student make a nature collection to show the class. She described kinds of things they might collect. Some students brought in their collections right away.

2   One collection was a box of interesting rocks. Another was a poster with leaves glued onto it. There was even a collection of snails in jars!

3   Marisa wanted to collect flowers, but she didn't want to pick them and press them. She didn't like to see them all flat and faded. She wanted to make a collection that would look as fresh and colorful as a garden.

4   Her first step was to search the neighborhood for the prettiest flowers. Next, she asked her neighbors the names of the flowers and how they cared for them. A few days later, Marisa displayed her collection for her class.

5   Marisa's flowers were as bright and pretty as the day she had found them. You see, Marisa had collected her flowers with a camera!

Use a Flow Chart to record the events in the story. Next to each event, write the number of the paragraph that tells that event. Then answer the questions below.

1. Which paragraphs tell the sequence of events? Which paragraphs explain or describe?

   _____

   _____

2. What event happened before Marisa brought her collection to school but is not explained until the end?

   _____

Action and Being Verbs

1–5. There is one action verb in each sentence. Write the verb on the line.

1. Randy finds words in a book. _____

2. His friends search for words everywhere. _____

3. His grandmother cut words from a letter. _____

4. Words hide in odd places. _____

5. Nobody kicked the box of words. _____

6–10. Write the being verb on the line. Write *present* or *past* for each verb.

6. Words are hard to find sometimes. _____

7. I am able to find words everywhere. _____

8. You were sweet to look for me. _____

9. We are tired of finding words. _____

10. The teachers were in their rooms with words. _____

More Short and Long Vowels

Write the Basic Words that match each heading.

Proper Nouns

1. _____

2. _____

Common Nouns

3. _____   7. _____

4. _____   8. _____

5. _____   9. _____

6. _____   10. _____

Describing Words

11. _____

12. _____

13. _____

Verb

14. _____

15–16: On the line below, write a sentence using one word from each group above.

_____

Spelling Words

Basic

1. math
2. toast
3. easy
4. socks
5. Friday
6. stuff
7. paid
8. cheese
9. June
10. elbow
11. program
12. shiny
13. piles
14. sticky

Review
each
both

Challenge
comb
holiday

Name _____ Date _____

Suffixes *-er* and *-or*

Write a sentence using the pair or group of words provided. Make sure the sentence helps the reader understand the meanings of the provided words. (You may add *-s* to these words.)

1. collector, traveler

_____

_____

2. pitcher, catcher, player

_____

_____

3. writer, illustrator

_____

_____

4. painter, director

_____

_____

5. buyer, seller

_____

_____

The Subject and the Predicate of a Sentence

- A sentence is a group of words that tells a complete thought and has a complete subject and a complete predicate.
- The subject tells whom or what the sentence is about and usually comes at the beginning of the sentence.
- The predicate tells what the subject does or is, and it can be one word or more than one word.

Many different words	*tell about the same idea.*
Subject	**Predicate**

1–2. Write the subject or the predicate of each sentence.

1. Tommy cut pictures from the newspaper. (subject) _____

2. He and his friends glued them to a poster. (predicate)

_____

3–4. Combine each pair of sentences. Use a compound subject in each new sentence. Write the new sentence on the line.

3. My friends gathered old clothes. The teachers gathered old clothes.

_____

4. The older kids carried the boxes. The parents carried the boxes.

_____

More Short and Long Vowels

Max's Words
Spelling:
More Short and Long Vowels

Find the misspelled words and circle them.

Jun 1: This was a great day! It started out like any other Frieday. I did all the usual stufe. I got dressed, put on my shoes and soks, and ate some tost and jam. But as I started to coamb my hair, I heard kids playing outside. For a minute, I thought it might be a holliday. Then suddenly I remembered that school is out. This is the first day of summer vacation! There are no more mathe tests, no more pils of homework, and no more long days of sitting still.

The rest of the day was perfect. I played kickball with my friends, rode my bike, and went to the pool. It was so much fun that I think I'll do it all again tomorrow. Or maybe I'll just watch TV and take it eazy. I <u>love</u> summer!

Spelling Words

1. math
2. toast
3. easy
4. socks
5. Friday
6. stuff
7. paid
8. cheese
9. June
10. elbow
11. program
12. shiny
13. piles
14. sticky

Review
each
both

Challenge
comb
holiday

Write the misspelled words correctly on the lines below.

1. _____   6. _____

2. _____   7. _____

3. _____   8. _____

4. _____   9. _____

5. _____   10. _____

Sentence Fluency

If the subject you are writing about is doing more than one action, you can tell about it in one sentence. You can combine more than one simple predicate to form a compound predicate. This can help make your sentences longer and less choppy.

Short Sentences with Simple Predicates	Longer, Smoother Sentence with Compound Predicate
Rick collects pictures of his friends. Rick puts them in a book.	Rick collects pictures of his friends and puts them in a book.
My father found nuts by a tree. My father put them in a bucket.	My father found nuts by a tree and put them in a bucket.

Combine each pair of sentences. Use a compound predicate in each new sentence. Write the new sentence on the line.

1. An old box was very dirty. An old box held many old pictures.

   _____

2. Harry found a picture of his grandfather. Harry put it in a frame.

   _____

3. Gregorio drew a picture of his aunt. Gregorio glued it to a board.

   _____

4. Grandma hid some photos in a drawer. Grandma found them later.

   _____

5. I found pictures in the basement. I brought them upstairs.

   _____

Write Words with Three-Letter Clusters

Read each question and choose an answer from the box. Write the word.

screwdriver	springtime	strongest
throne	scrubbing	unscramble
sprinkler	thrilling	streetlight

1. What do you call the person who can lift the heaviest

   load? _____

2. What lights the neighborhood on nights when there is no

   moon in the sky? _____

3. How would it feel to have an audience stand and applaud

   for you? _____

4. When do most seeds begin to sprout? _____

5. What helps grass grow when there is no rain? _____

6. What is kept in a toolbox and can help put things

   together? _____

7. What is the best way to get dirty hands clean?

   _____

8. What is a queen's chair called? _____

9. How can you make a word from a set of mixed-up

   letters? _____

Lesson 7
PRACTICE BOOK

Present and Past Tense

Many verbs in the **present tense** have an *-s* ending with a singular subject. Many verbs in the present tense do not have an *-s* ending with a plural subject. Most verbs in the **past tense** have an *-ed* ending.

Thinking Question
In what tense does the action of the verb occur, and what ending does the verb have?

An artist **paints** paintings.	present
Artists **paint** paintings.	present
An artist **painted** paintings yesterday.	past

**Write *present* if the underlined verb shows the present tense.
Write *past* if the underlined verb shows the past tense.**

1. Our class <u>gathers</u> pages for a book. _____

2. We <u>combined</u> them into a small book. _____

3. We <u>fold</u> some pages in two. _____

4. Other students <u>traced</u> lines for borders. _____

5. Carmen <u>cuts</u> the rough edges. _____

6. Walt and John <u>iron</u> the pages flat. _____

7. Some older kids <u>poked</u> holes in the page.

_____

8. One group <u>ties</u> string through the holes. _____

9. The string <u>pulled</u> the pages together. _____

10. In the last step, we <u>cover</u> it with thick paper.

_____

Text and Graphic Features

Read the selection below.

Planting Seeds for Stories

Nearly fifty years ago, Eric Carle started saving story ideas. When he had an idea, he made a scratch copy of the book it could become. Then one day, two ideas got the chance to become real books. A company wanted to publish *1, 2, 3 to the Zoo* and *The Very Hungry Caterpillar*!

Creating Pretty Papers

Eric Carle illustrated *The Very Hungry Caterpillar* with little pieces of cut paper. This kind of art is called **collage.** Since then, Carle has written many children's stories, all illustrated with bright, cut-paper pictures. To make pretty papers for his collages, Carle paints lines or wavy strokes of color on plain tissue paper. When the papers dry, he sorts them by color and stores them in drawers.

Working Magic with Scissors

To illustrate a story, Carle cuts out circles, squares, and other shapes from the colored papers. He arranges them to look like animals, stars, clouds, or whatever his story is about. Then he glues the pieces in place. When you look at the pictures in his stories, it's hard to believe they are all made from bits of paper!

Fun Facts!
1. It took two years for Eric Carle to finish *Do You Want to Be My Friend?* and only one week to complete *Little Cloud*!
2. Eric Carle has created more than seventy books for children.

Answer the questions.

1. Do you think the author made a good choice by including the list of Fun Facts? Why or why not? _____

2. What features could help you understand the reading better?

_____

Present, Past, and Future Tense

Verbs in the **future tense** use the helping verb *will*.
Many verbs in the **past tense** use an *-ed* ending.
Many verbs in the **present tense** with singular subjects
use an *-s* ending. Verbs in the present tense with
plural subjects do not use an ending.

The artist **paints** a curving line.	present
The artists **paint** a curving line.	present
The artist **painted** a curving line.	past
The artist **will paint** a curving line.	future

Thinking Question
*In what tense does
the action of the verb
occur, and what
ending does the
verb have?*

Write *present* if the underlined verb shows present tense. Write
past if the underlined verb shows past tense. Write *future* if the
underlined verb shows future tense.

1. My friends and I <u>walked</u> to the library. _____

2. We <u>will search</u> for fun picture books. _____

3. Lora <u>flips</u> through many books. _____

4. Kitty <u>stacked</u> the books that we liked. _____

5. Roberto and Vera <u>look</u> for the best ones. _____

6. Quentin <u>will place</u> a marker at the colorful ones.

   _____

7. Tory <u>loves</u> art with bright colors. _____

8. Walt <u>favors</u> art drawn with colored pencils. _____

Three-Letter Clusters

Write each Basic Word in the box where it belongs.

scr	*spr*
_____	_____
_____	_____
_____	_____
_____	_____

str	*thr*
_____	_____
_____	_____
_____	_____
_____	_____

Challenge Add the Challenge Words to your Word Sort.

Spelling Words

Basic
1. three
2. scrap
3. street
4. spring
5. thrill
6. scream
7. strange
8. throw
9. string
10. scrape
11. spray
12. threw
13. strong
14. scratch

Review
think
they

Challenge
straight
scramble

Name _____ Date _____

Focus Trait: Organization
Topic Sentence

A. Read the following paragraph. Decide if the paragraph compares or contrasts. Then complete the topic sentence with a connecting word.

1. Two illustrators have _____ drawing styles.

One draws with thick lines. The other lightly sketches

with pencil.

B. Read each paragraph. Decide if the paragraph compares or contrasts. Then write a topic sentence that clearly shows whether the paragraph compares or contrasts.

Pair/Share Work with a partner to think of connecting words.

2. Topic sentence: _____

_____

Most picture books have 32 pages. Novels, though, may have hundreds of pages.

3. Topic sentence: _____

_____

The main character of the first illustrator's book is a boy named Jack. The second illustrator drew pictures about a girl named Jacqueline.

Cumulative Review

Write words from the box to complete each paragraph.

threw	scratched	strong
screen	through	described
stretched	screamed	strange

Ray couldn't find the key to his house. He _____ his head
                                                                1
and tried to remember where he had seen it last. He went to the school

office and _____ his lost key chain. The clerk looked
                    2

_____ the Lost and Found box and found the key chain.
          3
Ray was grateful that someone had turned in his key!

***

Emily shivered as she looked out the window into the dark, foggy night.

Suddenly she heard a _____ noise coming from the back yard!
                                4
She tiptoed to the back of the house and pushed open the _____
                                                                          5
door. She heard someone pound on the house and say, "Boo!" Emily

_____. Then her brother stepped into the light and they both
        6
laughed.

***

There was once a troll so mean and so tough that no one in the village

was _____ enough to fight him. The villagers _____
          7   8
out a huge net on the ground and hid next to their houses. When the troll

came to town and stepped onto the net, the people wrapped him up, carried

him out of town, and _____ him into a big mud puddle. The
                              9
troll never came back!

Text and Graphic Features

Read the selection below.

Would you like to draw animals like the ones you see in cartoons? These steps will help you get started.

Look at a cartoon animal and try to see simple shapes in the drawing. With your finger, trace around the animal's face. Is it shaped like a circle or an oval? Draw a shape similar to the one you traced.

Do the same thing to decide the shape of the animal's other body parts. Add each shape to your drawing, overlapping them so each one is in the right position. Don't try to make the drawing look perfect.

When the "shape" sketch is finished, decide what you need to change or add. Erase any lines that you don't need. You can round pointed corners. Add straight lines or curves to show any other details you like.

Finally, trace the lines and curves of your drawing with a pen or fine-point marker.

Has your "ghost" turned into a cartoon? Congratulations! Maybe you will work as an illustrator someday!

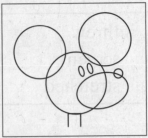

Make pencil shapes to show the "ghost" of a character.

Erase the lines where shapes overlap. Then add details.

Use a Column Chart to help you analyze the features. Then answer the questions.

1. Which features were most helpful to you in understanding the information in the article? Why?

_____

_____

2. How does the speech balloon in the last drawing connect the dog sketch to the information in the text?

_____

_____

Name _____ Date _____

Lesson 7
PRACTICE BOOK

What Do Illustrators Do?
Grammar:
Verb Tenses

Present, Past, and Future Tense

1–5. Write *present* if the underlined verb shows present tense.
Write *past* if the underlined verb shows past tense.

1. Bill, the artist, <u>selects</u> a wall for art. _____

2. He <u>looked</u> everywhere for a good wall. _____

3. Some kids <u>live</u> near this wall. _____

4. The owner <u>allowed</u> us to paint it. _____

5. Bill <u>climbs</u> on a tall ladder. _____

6–10. Write *present* if the underlined verb shows present tense.
Write *past* if the underlined verb shows past tense. Write *future* if
the underlined verb shows future tense.

6. The artist <u>will measure</u> the wall first. _____

7. The colors <u>drip</u> down the wall. _____

8. Someone else <u>painted</u> this wall long ago. _____

9. When it is done, people <u>will enjoy</u> the wall. _____

10. The new art <u>stretches</u> high into the sky. _____

Name _____ Date _____

Three-Letter Clusters

Write the Basic Word that is an antonym of the underlined word in each sentence.

1. Why did you choose such a <u>common</u> costume?
2. My uncle helped me learn how to <u>catch</u> a ball.
3. The <u>fall</u> is my favorite time of year.
4. Please <u>spread</u> the mud from your boots before coming in.
5. The surprise party was a big <u>bore</u> for me!
6. Are you <u>weak</u> enough to lift this heavy box?
7. Don't <u>whisper</u> in the library.
8. Everyone <u>caught</u> confetti to celebrate the new year.

1. _____   5. _____
2. _____   6. _____
3. _____   7. _____
4. _____   8. _____

Challenge: Write a word that means the opposite of each Challenge Word. Then use one of the Challenge Words and its antonym in a sentence.

9. _____

10. _____

11. _____

Spelling Words

Basic
1. three
2. scrap
3. street
4. spring
5. thrill
6. scream
7. strange
8. throw
9. string
10. scrape
11. spray
12. threw
13. strong
14. scratch

Review
think
they

Challenge
straight
scramble

Synonyms

sketch	large	see	enormous
view	show	illustrate	exhibit
polite	pleasant		

Read each word below. Write the two synonyms from above that have almost the same meaning as the word. Then write a sentence using one of the synonyms.

1. display

_____

_____

2. huge

_____

_____

3. nice

_____

_____

4. observe

_____

_____

5. draw

_____

_____

Kinds of Sentences

- There are four kinds of sentences.

The art is wonderful.	**Declarative** (statement)
Who made that piece?	**Interrogative** (question)
Pick up the mess you made.	**Imperative** (command)
What a bold color she used!	**Exclamatory** (exclamation)

1–3. Write *statement* if the sentence tells something. Write *question* if the sentence asks something.

1. We walked outside to paint. _____

2. Who is going to come with us? _____

3. Why are we going outside? _____

4–6. Write *command* if the sentence tells someone to do something. Write *exclamation* if the sentence shows strong feeling.

4. Painting outside is fun! _____

5. Do not spill paint out here. _____

6. Create a painting with bold colors. _____

Three-Letter Clusters

Find the misspelled words and circle them.

War of the Giants

Coming Soon!

In the sterange world of the future, giant animals roam the earth. But what happens when the beasts come together at the last city on Earth? See these thee monsters clash in the biggest battle of all time!

Birdzilla This giant bird has claws srong enough to skratch through solid rock. It is headed steraight for the city!

The Ape King When angry, this towering ape can lift a car off the steet and thow it into the air. People skream and run. But can they get away?

The Night Croc This huge crocodile waits at the edge of town. When you least expect it, he will sping out of the dark and attack. This movie is filled with thills and surprises.

Don't Miss It!

Spelling Words

1. three
2. scrap
3. street
4. spring
5. thrill
6. scream
7. strange
8. throw
9. string
10. scrape
11. spray
12. threw
13. strong
14. scratch

Review
think
they

Challenge
straight
scramble

Write the misspelled words correctly on the lines below.

1. _____   6. _____

2. _____   7. _____

3. _____   8. _____

4. _____   9. _____

5. _____   10. _____

Name _____ Date _____

Lesson 7
PRACTICE BOOK

Sentence Fluency

What Do Illustrators Do?
Grammar:
Connect to Writing

Keeping verbs in a paragraph in the same tense can avoid causing confusion.

Incorrect Paragraph

Next year, I will take an art class. Other students and I paint pictures of one another. We will study drawing and painting.

Correct Paragraph

Next year, I will take an art class. Other students and I will paint pictures of one another. We will study drawing and painting.

Read this paragraph. Change each underlined verb to make it match the tense of the other verbs. Write the new sentences on the lines below.

Maybe one hundred years from now, people will make new book covers. Books <u>flashed</u> lights. They will make noises. They <u>show</u> videos. Books will have movies in them. Readers <u>listened</u> to the words in the books. They will read them as well. Most of all, people <u>learn</u> from them. Kids <u>enjoy</u> these new types of books. The future of books will promise many wonderful things.

1. _____

2. _____

3. _____

4. _____

5. _____

Write Words with Silent Letters *kn*, *wr*

Read each line of the poem. Choose the missing word from the box. Write the word.

wring	wrists	knight
wrapped	knot	wrong
kneel	wrinkles	knee

Handy Things to Remember

To keep a gift a secret, keep it _____ and out of sight.
₁

To fight a pesky dragon, call a strong and fearless _____!
₂

If one string isn't long enough, get two and make a _____.
₃

To get the answers right, not _____, remember what you're
₄
taught.

To make a wet sponge dry, you need to _____ it out.
₅

Hold it tightly with both hands and twist your _____ about.
₆

Wear _____ pads when you're skating to keep from getting hurt.
₇

To look your best, make sure there are no _____ in your shirt.
₈

If you _____ in an anthill, stand up as quickly as you can.
₉

If you forget these handy tips, just read them all again!

Commas in a Series: Nouns

Use **commas** to separate three or more nouns together in a sentence. Commas tell readers when to pause.

Juan grew beans, corn, and tomatoes.

Thinking Question
Are there three or more nouns listed together in the sentence?

Write each sentence correctly. Add commas where they are needed.

1. Jamal Tina and Ed want to write their own folktales.

   _____

2. Their class is having a contest for plays poems and folktales.

   _____

3. The friends read stories on Monday Tuesday and Wednesday.

   _____

4. Jamal read folktales about crows fish and cats.

   _____

5. Tina likes the folktales of England Spain and Mexico.

   _____

6. Folktales can take place in deserts jungles and cities.

   _____

Conclusions

Read the selection. Then complete the Inference Map.

Long ago the Earth was warm all year round. The animals lived without a care. The wisest of the animals was a very old crow. His feathers shone with the colors of the rainbow, and his song was the sweetest of all the birds. Whenever the animals had a problem, they could always count on Rainbow Crow.

One day something strange began to fall from the sky. At first, the animals were curious about these tiny, white sparkling flakes, which kept falling and falling. Soon the animals did something they had never done before. They began to shiver and feel afraid. What was this strange whiteness that covered the fields and forests? The animals gathered together and called for Rainbow Crow. He heard their call and promised to help them.

Detail

Detail

Detail

Conclusion

Commas in a Series: Verbs

Use **commas** to separate three or more verbs together in a sentence.

> *Juan planted, watered, and harvested vegetables.*

Thinking Question
Are there three or more verbs listed in the sentence?

Write each sentence correctly. Add commas where they are needed. If no commas are needed, write *No Commas* on the line.

1. I plan write and correct my folktale.

_____

2. The animals in my story walk talk and snore.

_____

3. My friends listened laughed and clapped as I read my story.

_____

4. A snake trapped and tried to eat a frog in Ron's folktale.

_____

5. The frog danced jumped and ran away from the snake.

_____

Unexpected Consonant Spellings

Write each Basic Word in the web where it belongs.

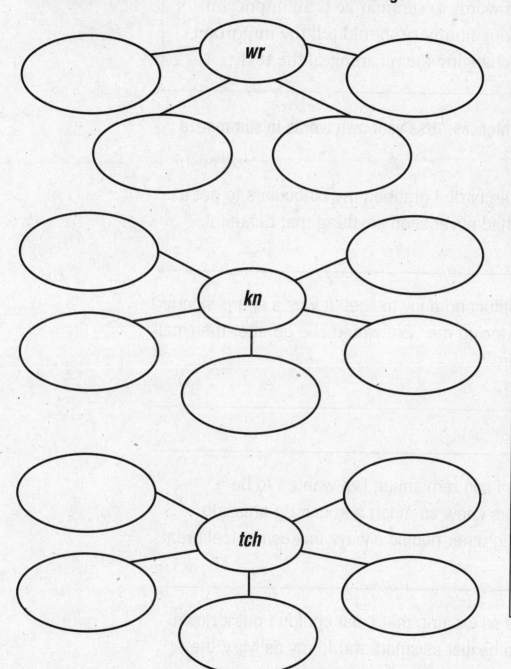

Spelling Words

Basic
1. itch
2. wreck
3. knee
4. patch
5. wrap
6. knot
7. watch
8. knife
9. stretch
10. write
11. knew
12. knock
13. match
14. wrong

Review
know
catch

Challenge
wrinkle
knuckle

Challenge: Add the Challenge Words to your Word Sort. Write each one near the correct group, and draw a line to connect it to the web.

Focus Trait: Word Choice
Using Your Own Words

> Using your own words to summarize is an important writing skill. Your summary should tell the important details without changing the meaning of the text.

Read each set of sentences. Use your own words to summarize the sentences.

1. At last, I saw the bird! I grabbed my binoculars to get a better look. I had never seen anything that beautiful.

   _____

2. She was beautiful and a joy to see! It was a sharp-skinned hawk, directly facing me. But would she go after the small birds in my yard?

   _____

   _____

3. For as long as I can remember, I've wanted to be a doctor. Doctors know so much and can do amazing things! Helping other people always makes me feel great.

   _____

4. The book was so exciting that I just couldn't put it down. I would like to be just as smart and funny as Max, the main character.

   _____

Cumulative Review

Write words from the box to complete the lines of the play.

know	wrong	wrote
threw	knees	through
knick-knacks	wrap	knocked

Granny and the Rascal

Granny Gopher: Who _____ over my beautiful vase?

Rascal Raccoon: Why are you so upset about a silly old vase? You have

plenty of other _____ sitting around.

Granny Gopher: That vase was special. Great-Granny Gopher gave it to

me. Now, is there something you'd like to confess?

Rascal Raccoon: I _____ that you think I broke that vase,

but I never went near it.

Granny Gopher: That's what you said after you _____ a

baseball _____ my window.

Rascal Raccoon: You were _____ about that, too.

Granny Gopher: There were witnesses to that crime. Skunk and Rabbit

_____ me a note saying they *saw* you break the window.

Rascal Raccoon: You can't trust what those tattle-tales say!

Granny Gopher: You can at least clean up this broken glass. It's hard for

me to get down on my sore old _____ to do a job like this.

Rascal Raccoon: Uh, sure, Granny Gopher. I have to go

_____ a present for Rabbit's birthday party right now. But I'll

stop by and help you later. *I promise!*

Lesson 8
PRACTICE BOOK

Conclusions

Read the story below.

Bernardo walked proudly through his cornfield. He was sure this year's harvest would bring a good price. He could use the money to buy a new pair of glasses. Suddenly, he noticed that several stalks had fallen over, and their ears of corn were ripped away. Bernardo saw large footprints on the ground. As he examined the damage, he shook his head and sighed. "Who would do such a terrible thing?" he wondered.

That night he kept watch from behind a tree near the field. As a cloud slipped past the moon, Bernardo spotted something sneaking toward the cornfield. Bernardo squinted through the scratched lenses of his glasses. He was sure it was his neighbor Carlos. "He has always been jealous of my luck," Bernardo thought. He stepped out from his hiding place. "I've caught you!" he shouted. The thief spun around. Bernardo gulped. It wasn't his neighbor. In fact, it wasn't human at all.

Use an Inference Map to help you draw a logical conclusion about what happened. Then answer the questions.

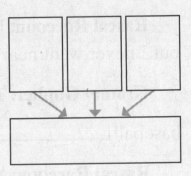

1. What conclusion did Bernardo draw about who was stealing his corn? Was that a logical conclusion? Why or why not?

_____

_____

_____

2. What do you conclude about why Bernardo was mistaken about the thief?

_____

_____

_____

Commas in a Series

1–5. Underline the series of nouns or verbs in each sentence.

1. Tia reads comics, poems, and plays.

2. Ralph, Jane, and Tom like funny folktales.

3. Birds talk, sing, and fight in one folktale.

4. Juan's cousins in Texas, Arizona, and Alaska like folktales.

5. All kinds of people like, read, and write folktales.

6–10. Write each sentence correctly. Add commas where they are needed.

6. Folktales stories and poems come from countries around the world.

_____

7. Some folktales come from Germany France and England.

_____

8. An animal in a folktale may talk fly or vanish.

_____

9. Animals in folktales often help hurt or tease people.

_____

10. Alice Bob and Teddy wrote folktales for class.

_____

Unexpected Consonant Spellings

Write the Basic Word that best completes each sentence.

1. Your elbow and your _____ are both body parts that can bend.

2. A pair of scissors and a _____ are both tools for cutting.

3. To share a story, you can tell it to someone or _____ it down.

4. Two things that can have a flame are a candle and a _____.

5. To tell the time, you can look at a clock or check your _____.

6. To let someone know you're at the door, ring the bell or _____.

7. You can tie a bow or just tie a _____.

8. A rubber band and bubble gum are both things that can _____.

Challenge: Name something that is similar to a knuckle. Then write to tell how the two things are alike.

9. _____

10. _____

_____

Spelling Words
Basic
1. itch
2. wreck
3. knee
4. patch
5. wrap
6. knot
7. watch
8. knife
9. stretch
10. write
11. knew
12. knock
13. match
14. wrong
Review
know
catch
Challenge
wrinkle
knuckle

Name _____ Date _____

Lesson 8
PRACTICE BOOK

The Harvest Birds
Vocabulary Strategies:
Multiple-Meaning Words

Multiple-Meaning Words

Read each sentence. Look up the underlined word in a
dictionary. Write the meaning that fits the way the word
is used in the sentence.

1. Did you <u>note</u> our meeting on your calendar?

_____

2. We needed another <u>yard</u> of streamers to decorate the
room.

_____

3. I didn't win, but I didn't feel <u>bitter</u> about it.

_____

4. She always hangs up her coat, so it was <u>odd</u> that she
misplaced it.

_____

Choose two of the underlined words from the sentences above.
Write a sentence that uses each word with a different meaning.

5. _____

6. _____

Sentence Fragments

- A sentence is a group of words that tells a complete thought. It tells who or what, and it tells what happens.

    A man planted seeds in his garden.

Write the group of words that will make a sentence.

1. A bird _____.

    lives in the tree   on the fence

2. Rabbits _____.

    soft and cute   like to eat garden vegetables

3. _____ are vegetable eaters.

    Rabbits   Usually

4. _____ ate the whole garden of flowers.

    Broke through a fence   A herd of goats

For each item, combine the two fragments to write a complete sentence.

5. A bird is. a clever but shy animal.

    _____

6. A garden needs. a fence that can keep animals out.

    _____

Unexpected Consonant Spellings

Find the misspelled words and circle them.

Lost Hiker Rescued on Big Pine Trail

Thanks to her own quick thinking, 8-year-old Rosa Gomez was rescued along Big Pine Trail on Saturday. The girl had stopped to wach a group of deer and became lost from her hiking group. She tried to catch up but took the rong trail. Rosa new she was lost and wanted to leave clues to help someone find her. She decided to rite her name in the dirt with a stick each time she took a turn. The girl had to stop after she fell on a rocky area. Her nuckles were scraped and her nee was badly cut. To stop the bleeding, Rosa used her pocket nife to cut a strip from her sweatshirt. She used the cloth to rap the injury and tie a not just as she had learned to do in first-aid training. The minutes began to strech into hours, but Rosa stayed calm. Rescuers found her just before dark.

Spelling Words

1. itch
2. wreck
3. knee
4. patch
5. wrap
6. knot
7. watch
8. knife
9. stretch
10. write
11. knew
12. knock
13. match
14. wrong

Review
know
catch

Challenge
wrinkle
knuckle

Write the misspelled words correctly on the lines below.

1. _____   6. _____

2. _____   7. _____

3. _____   8. _____

4. _____   9. _____

5. _____   10. _____

Sentence Fluency

You can combine short, choppy sentences to make your writing smoother. You can combine sentences by **joining single words in a series.** You use commas to separate the nouns or verbs in a series. Remember to add *and* after the last comma.

Short, Choppy Sentences	Longer, Smoother Sentence
Carla watched crows. Carla watched gulls. Carla watched pigeons.	Carla watched crows, gulls, and pigeons.

Combine three short, choppy sentences by joining nouns or verbs in a series. Write the new sentence on the line.

1.

The crows in the story walked.	The crows in the story laughed.	The crows in the story talked.

_____

2.

Carla told Ramon about the crows.	Carla told Ed about the crows.	Carla told Lisa about the crows.

_____

3.

The crows perched on branches.	The crows perched on wires.	The crows perched on rooftops.

_____

4.

Ramon played with the birds.	Ramon laughed with the birds.	Ramon flew with the birds.

_____

Words with Diphthongs
ow and *ou*

**Read each sentence. Choose the missing word from the box.
Write the word.**

crowded	rowdy	outdoors
found	showers	sunflower
howling	doghouse	shouted

1. As soon as the rain stopped, the children hurried

   _____ to play.

2. When a wolf is _____, you can hear it from
   far away.

3. Our poodle Fifi sleeps in her _____, where it
   is warm and dry.

4. When the birthday girl came in, everyone jumped up and

   _____, "Surprise!"

5. Will it be sunny today, or will we have _____?

6. The _____ seeds that we planted grew into
   tall plants with bright yellow blooms.

7. Carl still hasn't _____ the jacket that he lost
   last month.

8. The bus was so _____ that a lot of riders
   had to stand up.

9. If the children get too _____, they might
   wake the baby.

Nouns in the Subject

The subject of a sentence tells whom or what the sentence is about. The main word in the subject is often a **noun**. The main word is also called the **simple subject**.

The young man looked at the older one.

Thinking Question
What word in the subject tells whom or what the sentence is about?

The subjects in the sentences are underlined. On the blank lines, write the nouns, or simple subjects, that are in the subjects.

1. <u>My story</u> is about my bicycle ride. _____

2. <u>The bright sun</u> feels warm. _____

3. <u>My red bicycle</u> rides well. _____

4. <u>My dad's old tire</u> was flat. _____

5. <u>The brown seat</u> is soft. _____

6. <u>My legs</u> are tired. _____

7. <u>A basket</u> holds water bottles. _____

8. <u>Two new wheels</u> make the ride easy. _____

9. <u>A steep hill</u> is not easy to ride up. _____

10. <u>Riding</u> is fun! _____

Cause and Effect

Read the story. Then complete the T-Map. Include four causes and four effects.

One morning, an old man picked a peach from his tree. When he cut into it, he found a tiny baby. He and his wife raised the baby as their own son.

The boy never grew taller than an inch, but he was very strong and brave. Little One-Inch knew his parents were proud of him, but he wanted to prove himself to the world. He decided to travel to the emperor's palace.

The boy paddled down the river day after day. He faced rain, rough waters, and hungry fish, but he did not stop until he reached his goal.

At the palace, he introduced himself to the emperor. The emperor let the princess keep Little One-Inch as a playmate. That very day, a terrible ogre attacked the princess. Little One-Inch crawled into the shaggy hair covering the ogre's body and began to tickle him. The ogre giggled and squealed and rolled wildly about on the ground. Over and over he rolled until he rolled right into the river and sank to the bottom.

To thank Little One-Inch for his brave act, the emperor made him a samurai, an honored warrior.

Cause	Effect

Verbs in the Predicate

The predicate of a sentence tells what the subject does or is. The predicate can be one word or more than one word. The main word in the predicate is often a **verb**. It is also called a **simple predicate**.

> The storyteller _eats_ food.
> He _is_ a hungry person.

Thinking Question
What words in the predicate tell what the subject does or is?

The predicate in each sentence is underlined. Write the verb, or simple predicate, in each predicate on the line.

1. We hear a story. _____

2. The story is very funny. _____

3. It tells about a boy. _____

4. It lasts about an hour. _____

5. The teacher sits on the floor. _____

6. She talks about each person. _____

7. The boy in the story pushes a swing. _____

8. The girl on the swing moves through the air. _____

9. She goes very high. _____

10. She waves from the top. _____

Vowel Sound in *town*

Write each Basic Word in the list where it belongs.

m<u>ou</u>th	d<u>ow</u>n
_____	_____
_____	_____
_____	_____
_____	_____
_____	_____
_____	_____
_____	_____

Challenge Add the Challenge Words to your Word Sort.

Spelling Words

Basic
1. clown
2. round
3. bow
4. cloud
5. power
6. crown
7. thousand
8. crowd
9. sound
10. count
11. powder
12. blouse
13. frown
14. pound

Review
house
found

Challenge
mountain
coward

Focus Trait: Organization
Opinion Statement

When a question asks for your opinion, begin your answer by stating your opinion clearly. Use words from the question in your opinion statement.

EXAMPLE:

Question: In *Kamishibai Man*, why do you think the old man and his wife call each other "Grandma" and "Grandpa" although they have no children of their own?

Strong Opening: I think the old man and his wife call each other "Grandma" and "Grandpa" because they wish they had children and grandchildren.

Read each question about *Kamishibai Man*. Write a strong opening sentence that clearly states your opinion. Use words from the question.

1. **Question:** Why do you think the children were always happy to see the kamishibai man?

   Opinion Statement:

2. **Question:** How do you think the kamishibai man felt when he returned to the city?

   Opinion Statement:

3. **Question:** Why do you think the little boy ran away from the kamishibai man?

   Opinion Statement:

Cumulative Review

Write a word from the box to complete each rhyme.

clown	cow	kneel	pout	wreck
count	crown	knight	powder	write

1. You're going to have to _____ to change that wheel.

2. A princess wears a gown with her _____.

3. Please add some chili _____ to the chowder.

4. Why would you paint a frown on a _____?

5. You won't see that _____ lose a fight.

6. When you're dressed as a scout, do not _____.

7. The lady hurt her neck in the _____.

8. Be careful with that plow around the _____.

9. You should get this amount when you _____.

10. Before you start to _____, turn on a light.

Name _____ Date _____

Cause and Effect

Read the story below.

Lisa, Frank, and Granddad sat on the back porch eating watermelon.

"I used to raise watermelons," Granddad said. "Big ones, not itty-bitty melons like this one. You see, the soil on my farm was rich in dinosaur minerals. Thousands of dinosaurs were buried in a mudslide there a million years ago."

Frank was doubtful. He'd never heard of dinosaurs living in their area before.

"One year your grandma and I grew the biggest melon in the country," remembered Granddad. "I had to stand up on a ladder to climb up on top of it."

"Wow, that's really big!" said Lisa.

"That dinosaur dirt made everything big," Granddad said. "The green beans we used to grow were as long as my leg."

Lisa's mouth dropped open. "That soil was magic!" she said.

Granddad nodded. "You're right about that. We also had the best water in the country. It made our hens lay eggs the size of grapefruits. I gathered them with a wheelbarrow."

The thought of Granddad pushing a wheelbarrow full of giant eggs made Frank laugh. "You're just making up stories, right Granddad?"

"Well, call them stories if you like, but I call them memories," said Granddad with a wink. "Yes, sir. That's the way I remember it all."

Use a T-Map to show causes and effects. Then answer the questions.

1. Why doesn't Frank think Granddad's stories are true?

_____

_____

_____

2. Why does Lisa's mouth drop open?

_____

Simple Subjects and Simple Predicates

The subjects of the sentences are underlined. The predicates of the sentences are not underlined. Write the noun in the subject on one line and the verb in the predicate on the other line.

1. My friends enjoy this cooking story.

   Noun in the subject: _____

   Verb in the predicate: _____

2. Six young children mix flour and sugar.

   Noun in the subject: _____

   Verb in the predicate: _____

3. The hot oven has two trays in it.

   Noun in the subject: _____

   Verb in the predicate: _____

4. Bill's favorite cookie is a sugar cookie.

   Noun in the subject: _____

   Verb in the predicate: _____

5. The sister puts good food in the basket.

   Noun in the subject: _____

   Verb in the predicate: _____

6. The children eat dinner.

   Noun in the subject: _____

   Verb in the predicate: _____

Vowel Sound in *town*

Kamishibai Man
Spelling:
Vowel Sound in *town*

Write the Basic Word that best replaces the underlined word or words in each sentence.

1. The man wears a <u>ring of gold and jewels on his head</u> to show he is king.

2. The actress waved to the <u>large group of people</u> as she walked by.

3. The angry bees made a loud buzzing <u>noise</u>.

4. Her brother's teasing made Marta <u>put an unhappy look on her face</u>.

5. Let's <u>say the numbers in order</u> as Justin jumps the rope.

6. A <u>performer in a silly costume</u> gave out balloons to all the children.

7. That gray <u>puffy shape in the sky</u> looks like it might bring rain.

8. For my birthday, I had a <u>circle-shaped</u> cake decorated to look like a soccer ball.

1. _____ 5. _____

2. _____ 6. _____

3. _____ 7. _____

4. _____ 8. _____

Spelling Words

Basic
1. clown
2. round
3. bow
4. cloud
5. power
6. crown
7. thousand
8. crowd
9. sound
10. count
11. powder
12. blouse
13. frown
14. pound

Review
house
found

Challenge
mountain
coward

Challenge: On another sheet of paper, write a one-paragraph story using both Challenge Words and one or more Basic Words.

Lesson 9
PRACTICE BOOK

Kamishibai Man
Vocabulary Strategies:
Dictionary/Glossary Entry

Dictionary/Glossary Entry

Read each word. Find each word in a dictionary or glossary.
Complete the chart.

Word	Part(s) of Speech	Word with Endings	Number of Meanings
1. jewel			
2. rickety			
3. blast			
4. sharp			
5. blur			

Now write one sentence of your own that could be an example
sentence for one meaning of each word.

1. _____

2. _____

3. _____

4. _____

5. _____

Name _____ Date _____

Lesson 9
PRACTICE BOOK

Kamishibai Man
Grammar:
Spiral Review

Kinds of Nouns

- A noun that names any person, place, or thing is called a common noun.
- A noun that names a particular person, place, or thing is called a proper noun.
- Proper nouns begin with capital letters. A proper noun, like *Empire State Building*, may have more than one word.

  The old **man** was telling stories on **Elm Street**.

1–3. Identify the common nouns and proper nouns in the sentences and underline them. Then write the sentences correctly.

1. The crowd from the city was around jim molson.

_____

2. jim molson talked about the town of miami.

_____

3. Jim spoke about mitchell avenue.

_____

4–6. Write *common* or *proper* for the underlined nouns.

4. One man told a story about <u>America</u>. _____

5. A <u>woman</u> told a story about Columbus. _____

6. He sailed over the <u>Atlantic Ocean</u>. _____

Vowel Sound in *town*

Kamishibai Man
Spelling:
Vowel Sound in *town*

Find the misspelled words and circle them.

Dear Uncle Tony,

    Thanks for the circus tickets that you sent.
I can always cownt on you to make my birthday
a lot of fun! I really enjoyed the elephant act. The
biggest one must have weighed a thausand pownds.

    The acrobat show was great, too. No one made
a sownd while one acrobat carried his partner over
the tightrope. When they came down, they leaped
through a rownd hoop that was on fire. The crawd
went crazy! Then, a cloun pretended he was going
to do the same thing, but he was too scared. His
buddies laughed at him as if he was a big couward.
Finally, he jumped through the hoop and his pants
caught fire. When he took his bouw, he saw the
clowd of smoke behind him. It was really funny.

    I hope that next time you come to town, we can
all go to the circus together!

                        Love,
                        Gina

Spelling Words

1. clown
2. round
3. bow
4. cloud
5. power
6. crown
7. thousand
8. crowd
9. sound
10. count
11. powder
12. blouse
13. frown
14. pound

Review
house
found

Challenge
mountain
coward

Write the misspelled words correctly on the lines below.

1. _____
2. _____
3. _____
4. _____
5. _____
6. _____
7. _____
8. _____
9. _____
10. _____

Ideas

Adding a noun that tells more about another noun can make a sentence clearer. Put the added noun and any words that go with it right after the noun they tell about. Use a comma (,) before and after the words you add.

Without Added Words	With Added Words
Essie wants breakfast.	Essie, my best friend, wants breakfast.

Using the words in parentheses, write added words for the underlined sentences. Add commas before and after the added words.

Jen likes to tell a story about a family that gets a new TV set. Raul finds a new channel. (the son) He likes many different shows. Some of his favorite shows tell great stories. (such as movies) Raul and his dad love sports on television. They think the best football game is in January. (the Super Bowl) The whole family always watches this game. On Thanksgiving you'll also see them gathered around the TV set. (another big holiday)

1. _____

_____

2. _____

_____

3. _____

_____

4. _____

_____

Write Words with *au*, *aw*, *al*, and *o*

Read each sentence and choose an answer from the box. Write the word. Then read the sentence aloud.

tablecloth	yawning	offered
sauce	faucet	bossy
false	awesome	mall

1. To fill a water balloon, stretch the opening of the balloon

over a _____ and then turn on the water.

2. We went shopping at the _____ and

had lunch at the Food Court.

3. My _____ cousin Cindy makes her

brothers do everything her way.

4. Pete had two scoops of ice cream with chocolate

_____ and whipped cream on top.

5. On our test, we had to tell whether each statement was

true or _____.

6. The desert sunset was an _____ sight!

7. Coach Simms _____ to help me work on my pitch.

8. The gravy spilled and stained our best _____.

9. Are the girls _____ because they are

tired or because they are bored?

Name _____ Date _____

Subject Pronouns

A **pronoun** is a word that can take the place of one or more nouns in a sentence. The pronouns *I, you, he, she, it, we,* and *they* are **subject pronouns**. Pronouns can be singular or plural. A noun and the subject pronoun that replaces it must match each other in singular and plural forms.

> *The telegraph was important.*   *It was important.*
> *Samuel Morse invented it.*   *He invented it.*
> *Our class learned this.*   *We learned this.*

Thinking Question
What pronoun can replace and match a noun or nouns in a sentence?

Write each sentence. Replace the underlined word or words with a subject pronoun.

1. <u>Samuel Morse</u> was born in Massachusetts.

   _____

2. <u>Lucretia Walker</u> became his wife.

   _____

3. <u>The couple</u> had two children.

   _____

4. <u>Painting</u> was another thing Morse did well.

   _____

5. <u>The students and I</u> enjoyed learning about him.

   _____

Name _____ Date _____

Lesson 10
PRACTICE BOOK

Young Thomas Edison
Introduce Comprehension:
Main Ideas and Details

Main Ideas and Details

**Read the selection. Underline the main idea and
look for supporting details. Then complete the Idea-Support Map.**

Hedy Lamarr was a famous actress. She starred in twenty-five
films. But that's not all that made her a star. This beautiful actress was
also a great inventor.

In the 1940s, America was at war with Germany. Hedy came up with
a clever idea. It was a way to send secret radio messages. The system
used radio waves in a special way. It made the waves keep changing so
enemies couldn't pick up the signal. The code was unbreakable! Hedy
gave her idea to her country at no cost. It was too late to help in the war
with Germany, but it did help America in later wars.

Lamarr has had a big effect on today's world. Her idea for using
radio waves has made cell phones, fax machines, and the scanner at the
checkout stand possible. As an inventor, Hedy is still a star today!

Object Pronouns

The pronouns *me*, *you*, *him*, *her*, *it*, *us*, and *them* are called **object pronouns**. Object pronouns follow action verbs and words like *to*, *for*, *at*, *of*, and *with*. A noun and the object pronoun that replaces it must match each other in singular and plural forms.

- The pronouns *it* and *you* are both subject pronouns and object pronouns.

> *Nikola Tesla helped invent radio.*
> *Nikola Tesla helped invent it.*
>
> *Others worked with Tesla.*
> *Others worked with him.*

Thinking Question
What pronoun replaces and matches one or more nouns that are the objects in a sentence?

Write each sentence. Replace the underlined word or words with an object pronoun.

1. A man named Marconi worked on wireless communication.

_____

2. He helped make radios popular.

_____

3. Marconi married Beatrice O'Brien in 1905.

_____

4. Other people said they had invented the system.

_____

5. People are grateful to Marconi for what he did.

_____

Vowel Sound in *talk*

Write each Basic Word where it belongs in the chart.

soft	paw
_____	_____
_____	_____
_____	_____
_____	_____
_____	_____

fall
_____
_____
_____
_____

Challenge: Add the Challenge Words to your Word Sort.

Spelling Words

Basic
1. talk
2. cross
3. awful
4. law
5. cloth
6. cost
7. crawl
8. chalk
9. also
10. raw
11. salt
12. wall
13. lawn
14. always

Review
soft
small

Challenge
often
strawberry

Focus Trait: Sentence Fluency
Avoiding Redundancy

Good writers introduce a new idea in each sentence. This writer crossed out a sentence that repeats an idea and wrote a new idea.

Thomas Edison loved to read. He would spend the entire day at the library. He wanted to read every book in the library. He would start at the last book on the shelf and work back to the first. ~~Edison wanted to read all of the books there~~.

New idea: *He would dream about his next experiment as he read.*

Read each paragraph. Cross out the sentence that repeats an idea. Write a new idea.

1. Thomas Edison was a very creative child. He created a laboratory in the cellar of his home. He would mix chemicals there. He would do this in the cellar. He also asked questions so that he could learn about things.

   New Idea: _____

2. Edison's mother was important in his life. She educated him at home. She taught him very well there. She also encouraged him to learn for himself.

   New Idea: _____

3. Edison invented many helpful things. He invented the carbon transmitter, which made voices sound louder. He invented the light bulb. This invention helped people. He even invented the motion picture.

   New Idea: _____

   _____

Cumulative Review

Write words from the box to complete the sentences.

cause	walkie-talkies	squawked
officer	foggy	already
paws	fault	flossing

1. My friend and I used _____ to communicate.

2. Brushing and _____ keep teeth healthy.

3. The chicken _____ loudly and flapped

her wings.

4. Why did the police _____ question that man?

5. Dr. Ross finally figured out the _____ of

the baby's fever.

6. When Tasha arrived, the game had

_____ started.

7. It was so _____ that I could barely see

my neighbor's house.

8. It was my _____ that the library book

got torn.

9. The kitten is all black except for its four white

_____.

Name _____ Date _____

Main Ideas and Details

Read the passage below. Infer the main idea by thinking about what connects details in the text.

Young George Nissen was at the circus when he got a great idea. George was a gymnast and had come to see the trapeze artists. At the end of the act, the acrobats dropped into a safety net that sent them bouncing high into the air. Nissen thought the net would be great for practicing gymnastics. It looked like fun, too!

George was not just a daydreamer. At age sixteen, he put together a rectangular frame made of steel from a junkyard. Then he stretched a piece of canvas cloth over it. He fastened the cloth with strips cut from old rubber inner tubes. He took his invention to a camp where he worked as a counselor. The kids loved bouncing on it!

George saw an opportunity and grabbed it. He and some friends took the bouncing rig on the road. They performed at schools all over the country. People saw how much fun they were having and wanted to buy their own bouncing rig. That's when George decided to name his invention. He called it the trampoline!

Use an Idea-Support Map to record supporting details and the main idea. Then answer the questions.

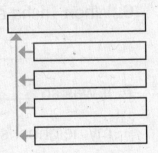

1. What details support the statement, "George was not just a daydreamer"?

_____

_____

_____

2. What did George do to make his idea a success?

_____

_____

Subject and Object Pronouns

**Write each sentence. Replace the underlined word or words
with a subject pronoun.**

1. <u>Raul and Kevin</u> think about inventing.

   _____

2. <u>Pauline</u> helped to type their ideas.

   _____

3. Then everyone said, "<u>All of us</u> are done with this invention!"

   _____

4. Ms. Jones said, "<u>Ms. Jones</u> thought you did well!"

   _____

**Write each sentence. Replace the underlined word or words with
an object pronoun.**

5. Kevin wanted to sell <u>his invention book</u>.

   _____

6. A man outside bought the book for <u>his daughter</u>.

   _____

7. A teacher asked <u>Kevin</u> what he was doing.

   _____

8. Then Kim said, "Show <u>Kim</u> the book!"

   _____

Vowel Sound in *talk*

Read the titles and lists below. Write the Basic Word that belongs in each blank.

1. Things to Look for Before You _____: cars, trucks, bicycles

2. Ways to Communicate: draw a picture, use sign language, _____

3. Writing Tools: pencil, pen, _____

4. Things That Are Against the _____: littering, speeding, stealing

5. Spices and Seasonings: garlic, cinnamon, _____

6. Things People Eat _____: apples, lettuce, tomatoes

7. Parts of a Building: staircase, window, _____

8. Things Made of _____: shirt, scarf, sheet

Challenge: Write two lists similar to those above. Include a Challenge Word in each title or list.

Spelling Words

Basic
1. talk
2. cross
3. awful
4. law
5. cloth
6. cost
7. crawl
8. chalk
9. also
10. raw
11. salt
12. wall
13. lawn
14. always

Review
soft
small

Challenge
often
strawberry

Name _____ Date _____

Lesson 10
PRACTICE BOOK

Young Thomas Edison
Vocabulary Strategies:
Categorize and Classify

Categorize and Classify

Categorize by adding a title to each list. Classify by adding one word that belongs in each list.

_____

astronomer

chemist

geologist

_____

_____

bones

blood

muscles

_____

_____

rain

snow

hail

_____

_____

desert

rain forest

ocean

_____

Singular and Plural Nouns

> • A noun that names only one person, place, or thing is a **singular noun**.
>
> • A noun that names more than one person, place, or thing is a **plural noun**.
>
> • Add *-s* to most singular nouns to form the plural.
>
> • Add *-es* to form the plural of a singular noun that ends in *-s*, *-sh*, *-ch*, or *-x*.
>
> > Students have invented <u>things</u> for many of their school <u>classes</u>.

1–5. Write singular or plural for each underlined noun.

1. An <u>invention</u> is like a lightbulb lighting up in your head.

_____

2. Before, my <u>thoughts</u> were in the dark. _____

3. I don't know how a new <u>idea</u> comes to me. _____

4. I phoned two <u>friends</u> about my idea. _____

5. I will give them two <u>guesses</u> about what it is.

_____

6–10. Use proofreading marks to change the underlined nouns from singular nouns to plural nouns.

Thank you for the <u>idea</u> <u>box</u> that you sent. We should meet to talk about

the <u>invention</u> we are thinking about. I shared your <u>thought</u> with my <u>brother</u>.

Vowel Sound in *talk*

Find the misspelled words and circle them.

This morning was auful. I wanted to sleep late, but my brother kept whining. He was crawss because Mom wouldn't let him go out and play unless I went with him. I olways have to babysit! All I wanted was a little sleep. Since when is that against the lauw? Anyway, I took Ben out to play. I stretched out on the laun to relax, but before long Ben just had to crol over and bug me. He doesn't tawk very well yet, but I know what "jump game" means. Ben auften watches me play hopscotch and thinks it looks funny. I got some chawk and drew a board on the sidewalk. Ben laughed when I hopped on the squares. Then he was bored again. He wanted to swing. He aulso wanted a drink of water. When Ben finally took his nap, I ran to Ana's house. I'm going to sleep over tonight. Maybe I'll get to sleep late at HER house!

Spelling Words

Basic
1. talk
2. cross
3. awful
4. law
5. cloth
6. cost
7. crawl
8. chalk
9. also
10. raw
11. salt
12. wall
13. lawn
14. always

Review
soft
small

Challenge
often
strawberry

Write the misspelled words correctly on the lines below.

1. _____   6. _____

2. _____   7. _____

3. _____   8. _____

4. _____   9. _____

5. _____   10. _____

Sentence Fluency

Using a pronoun in place of a noun helps you to not repeat the same nouns over and over.

Repeated Nouns	Better Sentences
In 1806, Thomas Young thought of the phonograph. Later, Leon Scott improved the phonograph. Thomas Edison made the phonograph work.	In 1806, Thomas Young thought of the phonograph. Later, Leon Scott improved it. Thomas Edison made it work.

Rewrite each item. Use pronouns in place of repeated nouns.

1. The first phonograph did not play records. The first phonograph put sounds on a tin tube. Sounds entered the first phonograph through a bell.

   _____

   _____

2. Later, phonographs played records. These records were flat rings of wax. A needle cut sound into the records.

   _____

   _____

3. Bell and Tainter made their phonograph in 1886. Bell and Tainter called their phonograph a gramophone. The government gave its approval to Bell and Tainter.

   _____

   _____

Words with Vowel Diphthongs *oi, oy*

Read each sentence. Choose the missing word from the box.
Write the word. Then reread the complete sentence.

broiling	ointment	soy
coiled	oyster	disappoint
voyage	avoid	hoist

1. While hiking, Debra saw a snake _____ up on the path.

2. Before you can go sailing, you have to

   _____ the sails.

3. Steve made sure to get his mom a birthday card so that

   he would not _____ her.

4. My bike has a flat tire because I did not

   _____ the broken glass on the sidewalk.

5. Christine cooked the hotdogs by _____ them.

6. My grandmother is making a _____ around the world.

7. I don't like seafood, so I did not eat the _____.

8. Gwen put some _____ on her poison ivy rash.

9. My mom eats burgers that are made with

   _____ instead of meat.

Changing *y* to *i*

- Add *-s* or *-es* to most nouns to form the **plural**.
- If a noun ends with a consonant and *y*, change the *y* to *i*, and add *-es* to form the plural.

  Singular: family   party

  Plural: families   parties

Thinking Question
Does the noun end with a consonant and y?

Write the plural form of each singular noun in parentheses.

1. My teammates and I play basketball in many _____. (city)

2. We once played against a team that had _____ on their shirts. (pony)

3. Another team had two _____ on their shirts. (butterfly)

4. The teams are not really _____. (enemy)

5. I made _____ of the photos I took of the games. (copy)

Name _____ Date _____

Lesson 11
PRACTICE BOOK

Jump!
Introduce Comprehension:
Fact and Opinion

Fact and Opinion

Read the selection.

Last summer, my family visited New York City. I think it was the best trip I've ever taken.

Before we went, I spent a lot of time learning about the city. New York City is the largest city in the United States. It is home to over eight million people!

On our trip, we stayed in Manhattan. Manhattan is an island. It is only about thirteen miles long and about two miles wide. It is amazing that such a small place can have so much to offer.

When we arrived, the city was buzzing. I loved the energy of the place right away. That night, we saw a Broadway show.

The next day, we visited the Bronx Zoo. It is the largest zoo in a city anywhere in the United States.

I believe that everyone should visit New York City. It is home to incredible restaurants, museums, and people.

Use the chart to write facts and opinions from the selection.

Facts	Opinions

Special Plural Nouns

- The spelling of some plural nouns changes in a special way.

  The <u>woman</u> wanted to be as tall as other <u>women</u>.
- The spelling of some nouns does not change when they are plural.

  That black <u>sheep</u> is as large as all the other <u>sheep</u>.
- The noun *woman* is *women* when it is plural.
- The noun *sheep* is *sheep* when it is plural.

Thinking Question
Does the noun add -s or -es, or does it change its spelling? Does its spelling not change?

Write the plural form of the noun in parentheses to complete each sentence.

1. Tara grew up to be stronger than most other _____. (woman)

2. She was taller than most of the other _____ her age. (child)

3. As she grew, she could run faster than most _____. (deer)

4. Every fall she ran through the _____. (leaf)

5. She ran and won many races against _____. (man)

6. She had a bright smile filled with white _____. (tooth)

Name _____ Date _____

Vowel Sound in *joy*

Write each Basic Word under the correct heading.

Vowel Sound in *joy* spelled *oi*	Vowel Sound in *joy* spelled *oy*
_____	_____
_____	_____
_____	_____
_____	_____
_____	_____
_____	_____
_____	_____
_____	_____
_____	_____
_____	_____

Challenge: Add the Challenge Words to your Word Sort.

Spelling Words

Basic
1. joy
2. point
3. voice
4. join
5. oil
6. coin
7. noise
8. spoil
9. toy
10. joint
11. boy
12. soil
13. choice
14. boil

Review
come
are

Challenge
poison
destroy

Focus Trait: Word Choice
Sensory Words and Details

Good writers use sensory words—words that let readers see, hear, smell, taste, and touch—and vivid details to paint a clear picture of what they are trying to say. Compare the sentence without sensory words and details to the one with sensory words and details.

Without Sensory Words and Details: Erin won the game.

With Sensory Words and Details: Erin crushed the last pitch and rounded the bases to win the game.

Rewrite each sentence, adding sensory words and details. You may use the words in the box for ideas and then add words or phrases of your own.

Sensory Words				
old	booming	tiny	rumbled	thud

1. The car went down the road.

_____

2. Anna fell.

_____

3. The snow fell all day.

_____

4. The chair broke.

_____

5. He called my name.

_____

Cumulative Review

Write a word from the box to complete each sentence. Then read the complete sentence.

royal	cowboy	pointy
enjoy	avoid	voyage
oiled	loyal	noisy

1. The men working outside my window were so

_____ that I could not fall asleep.

2. Theresa is a _____ friend, so I know I can
trust her.

3. Marc knew that his trip around the world would be the

_____ of a lifetime.

4. The metal lid was rusted shut because no one had

_____ it for years.

5. A king and a queen are _____ rulers.

6. Victor is mad at me, so I will _____ talking
to him at school.

7. If you _____ funny movies, you will love
this one!

8. Once I get some fake _____ ears, my elf
costume will be complete.

9. Randy loved taking horseback riding lessons because it

made him feel like a _____.

Fact and Opinion

Read the selection below.

Babe Ruth was the greatest baseball player in history. However, his childhood did not point to greatness. George Herman "Babe" Ruth was born in Baltimore, Maryland, in 1895. His parents worked very hard. They wanted him to have more than they could give him. When George was seven, his parents sent him to live at St. Mary's Industrial School.

At first, St. Mary's seemed like the worst place in the world. However, there was a priest there named Brother Matthias. He realized that George just needed someone to guide him. Brother Matthias taught George how to behave and to play baseball.

George loved baseball. He was a great hitter but an even better pitcher. In 1914, the owner of the Baltimore Orioles met George. He offered George a job playing baseball. George was just 19. His teammates thought he looked very young. They gave him the nickname "Babe." The name stuck for the rest of his life.

Use a T-Map to record four facts and four opinions from the selection. Then answer the questions.

1. The passage says that Babe Ruth began playing for the Baltimore Orioles when he was 19. Is this a fact or an opinion? How do you know?

_____

_____

2. Imagine you were one of Ruth's teammates in 1914. Could you have disagreed that Ruth looked very young? What does this tell you about the sentence, "His teammates thought he looked very young?"

_____

_____

Special Plural Nouns

1–5. Write the plural form of each singular noun in parentheses.

1. two tiny _____ (baby)

2. four long _____ (story)

3. twelve ripe _____ (cherry)

4. fresh red _____ (berry)

5. eight cute _____ (puppy)

6–10. Write *singular* or *plural* for each underlined noun.

6. Many <u>women</u> play sports. _____

7. Many <u>men</u> take part in sports, too. _____

8. Jack wore a guard to protect his <u>teeth</u>. _____

9. A <u>child</u> can play sports at school. _____

10. <u>Geese</u> do not play sports. _____

Vowel Sound in *joy*

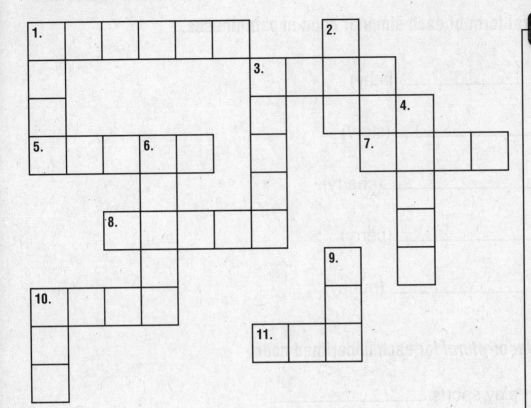

Spelling Words

Basic
1. joy
2. point
3. voice
4. join
5. oil
6. coin
7. noise
8. spoil
9. toy
10. joint
11. boy
12. soil
13. choice
14. boil

Review
come
are

Challenge
poison
destroy

Use the Basic Words to complete the puzzle.

Across
1. a decision
3. to become a member
5. a sound
7. dirt
8. a small dot
10. to heat a liquid until it bubbles
11. great happiness

Down
1. a metal piece of money
2. a black, slippery liquid
3. the place where two bones connect
4. what one uses to speak
6. to go bad
9. something to play with
10. a male child

Suffixes -y, -ful, -ous

In each sentence, circle the word with the suffix
-y, -ful, or -ous. Then write the base word, the suffix, and the
word meaning. Use context clues in the sentence to help you
find the meaning.

1. Uncle Mario is a skillful carpenter who can build just about anything out

   of wood.

   _____   _____   _____
   base word   **suffix**   **meaning**

2. Gloria's eyes got big when she took a bite of the peppery stew.

   _____   _____   _____
   base word   **suffix**   **meaning**

3. My grandmother is an adventurous person who likes to see new places

   and try new things.

   _____   _____   _____
   base word   **suffix**   **meaning**

4. It is hard to say no to our coach because he is such a powerful person.

   _____   _____   _____
   base word   **suffix**   **meaning**

5. Our dog Red came home covered with slimy mud after playing in the creek.

   _____   _____   _____
   base word   **suffix**   **meaning**

Kinds of Verbs

- A word that tells what people or things do is a **verb**. Words that show action are **action verbs**.

- Some verbs do not show action. They are **being verbs**. The verbs *am*, *is*, *are*, *was*, and *were* are forms of the verb *be*. They tell what someone or something is or was.

    The players <u>jump</u>, and they <u>are</u> strong.

1–3. Identify the underlined verb in each sentence. Write *action* or *being* on the line.

1. Tammy <u>worked</u> hard for the race. _____

2. She <u>was</u> a weak runner. _____

3. Her coach <u>taught</u> her exercises. _____

4–6. Combine each pair of sentences. Use both verbs in the new sentence. Write the new sentence on the line.

4. Jena jumped four feet high. Jena landed in the foam pit.

_____

5. The team hopped around the track. The team was soon tired.

_____

6. The coaches were impressed. The coaches were happy.

_____

Proofread for Spelling

Jump!
Spelling:
Vowel Sound in *joy*

Circle the ten misspelled Spelling Words in the following letter. Then write each word correctly.

Dear Louise,

I hope that you are doing well. I wish that I could jion you this week at camp. Sadly, I've lost my voic, so Mom says I have to rest. Sitting inside while everyone else has fun definitely wouldn't be my choyce. Boiy am I bored! I did get a cool new toi, though. It is a tiny robot that makes this weird noyse whenever you poiynt a light at it. I think Dad wants to destroiy it already. He thinks playing with it is like poyson to my brain and says I should read more books. He's probably right. Oh, I also got this neat old coyn from my grandfather. Anyway, write back when you can!

Your friend,

Albert

Spelling Words

Basic
1. joy
2. point
3. voice
4. join
5. oil
6. coin
7. noise
8. spoil
9. toy
10. joint
11. boy
12. soil
13. choice
14. boil

Review
come
are

Challenge
poison
destroy

1. _____   6. _____

2. _____   7. _____

3. _____   8. _____

4. _____   9. _____

5. _____   10. _____

Conventions: Proofreading

If a noun ends with a consonant and *y*, change the *y*
to *i*, and add *-es* to form the plural.

Sometimes the spelling of a noun changes in a special way.

The spelling of some nouns does not change when they
are plural.

Incorrectly Formed Plural	Correctly Formed Plural
cherry cherrys	cherry cherries
goose gooses	goose geese
deer deers	deer deer

**Proofread the paragraph. Find five mistakes in the spelling of
plural nouns. Write the corrected sentences on the lines below.**

> The mans on the ski team learned a lot from the women. They
> showed them how to relax and go faster. They told them storys about
> great women skiers.
>
> On top of the mountain, the skiers saw deers. They had to be careful
> not to run into them. Two women fell on the way down. Their familys
> were worried. But they were all right. Now they don't have any worrys.

1. _____

2. _____

3. _____

4. _____

5. _____

Write Homophones

Read each sentence. Choose the missing word from
the box. Write the word. Then reread the complete sentence.

chews	mail	heal
choose	cent	heel
male	sent	he'll

1. A stallion is a _____ horse.

2. The poor man didn't have a _____ on him.

3. That wound should _____ in a few days.

4. Becky's shoe was loose at the _____.

5. Ernesto always _____ his food slowly.

6. Ginger's uncle _____ her a birthday present.

7. Watch for an important letter in the _____.

8. It is hard to _____ between two of your
favorite foods.

9. If the cat doesn't like his food, _____
complain.

Names for People and Animals

- Nouns that name a particular person, pet, or family member are called **proper nouns**. Always begin a proper noun with a capital letter.
- Begin a family name or an initial in a name with a capital letter.
- A family name begins with a capital letter only when it is used in place of a person's name.

  Is <u>Grandpa</u> coming with <u>Tom</u>?

  <u>John F. Kennedy</u> was a great man.

Thinking Question
Is the word the name of a particular person, pet, family member, or an initial in a name?

Two nouns in each sentence are underlined. Find the proper noun, and write it correctly.

1. Gregorio's family went to visit the <u>house</u> of <u>mary j. renson</u>.

   _____

2. She trained <u>cowboys</u> and <u>trigger</u>, her pony. _____

3. I think <u>father</u> hopes that this <u>woman</u> will help us. _____

4. Mrs. <u>renson</u> will help our <u>animals</u>. _____

5. A <u>man</u> named <u>david</u> works with all kinds of pets. _____

6. He will teach our cat <u>lulu</u> to do <u>tricks</u>. _____

7. Our other <u>pets</u> go to <u>doctor gray</u> to learn, too. _____

8. One of the <u>hamsters</u> was named <u>phineas t. barnum</u>. _____

Story Structure

Read the selection. Then complete the Story Map.

Robby was trembling in his seat in the school gym. The principal was about to announce the winners in the science essay contest. Students had to write about why science was important to them. The grand prize was a trip to the Smithsonian Museums.

Robby really wanted to go on the trip, but he felt that his essay was not very good. Robby had not liked science before the contest. But when he started brainstorming ideas, he discovered that he really did find science interesting.

The principal announced the third prize winner, who went up to receive her certificate. Then, the second prize winner went up to get his prize, a chemistry set. Then, the principal announced the winner: Robert Price. It took a moment for Robby to realize the principal had called his name! Robby's essay was good after all, and he would go to Washington!

Characters	Setting
Plot	

Names for Places

Thinking Question
Is the noun the name of a particular place?

- A noun that names a particular place is a proper noun. Particular places include streets, cities and towns, states, countries, schools, parks, rivers, and lakes. Names of particular places begin with a capital letter.

- Each important word in a proper noun begins with a capital letter. Do not begin *of* or *the* with a capital letter.

    My family came from Mexico near the Sea of Cortez.

- Remember to include a comma between the name of a city and a state.

    Kevin is from Dayton, Ohio.

Two nouns in each sentence are underlined. Find the proper noun and write it correctly.

1. Gina helped people who came from ireland. _____

2. She lived in a town near springfield, massachusetts.

    _____

3. Gina baby-sat their children in darlington park. _____

4. Many of the women had come from the city of dublin. _____

5. Some lived in houses along the river liffey. _____

6. Their sons and daughters now attend king elementary school.

    _____

Name _____ Date _____

Lesson 12
PRACTICE BOOK

The Science Fair
Spelling:
Homophones

Homophones

Write Basic Words to answer the following questions.

1. Which two words use the same vowel sound as *air*?

   _____, _____

2. Which two words use the same vowel sound as *ear*?

   _____, _____

3. Which two words use the same vowel sound as *burn*?

   _____, _____

4. Which two words use the same vowel sound as *once*?

   _____, _____

5. Which two words use the same vowel sound as *go*?

   _____, _____

6. Which two words use the same vowel sound as *in*?

   _____, _____

7. Which two words use the same vowel sound as *now*?

   _____, _____

Challenge Write two sentences. Use one Challenge Word in each sentence.

1. _____

2. _____

Spelling Words

Basic
1. hole
2. whole
3. its
4. it's
5. hear
6. here
7. won
8. one
9. our
10. hour
11. their
12. there
13. fur
14. fir

Review
road
rode

Challenge
peace
piece

Focus Trait: Word Choice
Onomatopoeia

Onomatopoeia is the use of words whose sounds make you think of their meanings. They are sound effect or noise words, such as *Boom! Crack! Thud!* Using onomatopoeia can add voice, life, and humor to your writing.

Think about sounds you have heard on the way to school, inside or outside the classroom, or during a thunderstorm. Using the words below, write five sentences describing those sounds.

bark, blare, boom, buzz, chirp, clang, clatter, click, crash, drip, giggle, growl, hiss, honk, meow, moan, ouch, plop, plunk, purr, rattle, slap, squeak, squeal, squish, swoosh, wham, whizz

1. _____

_____

2. _____

_____

3. _____

_____

4. _____

_____

5. _____

_____

Words Ending in *-er, -le*

Write a word from the box to complete each sentence in the story. Then read the complete sentence.

bottle	ladle	table
dreamer	longer	teacher
kettle	sweeter	warmer

1. "Wake up, _____!" my mom calls every morning.

2. "Can't I sleep a little _____?" I always ask.

3. Soon I am in the kitchen, where it is _____ and full of action.

4. The _____ is already set for breakfast.

5. I get the _____ of milk from the refrigerator.

6. In a few minutes the tea _____ sings, saying the water is ready.

7. I love making Mom's tea for her. "Just a bit more honey, to make it _____," I say.

8. Then I watch as Dad puts a _____ full of oatmeal in my favorite bowl. Yum!

9. He wraps up a muffin, smiles, and winks. "Give this to your _____ before school today."

Story Structure

Read the selection.

It was the night of the school talent show. Andreia was backstage looking for her friends Kofi and Jin to give them their costumes. She felt nervous: What if their play wasn't interesting enough? When she finally found Kofi, he looked worried. "Jin had to go home sick!" he cried, "What will we do?"

Just then, Andreia noticed a large dummy in the corner. She handed Kofi his costume and disappeared into the dressing room with the dummy. When she came out, the dummy was in Jin's costume! Kofi looked confused. Andreia explained, "We'll have to do this play without Jin. Here! This dummy will be his character!"

They went out on stage and began the play. The dummy was so ridiculous, the audience thought the play was a comedy. Kofi and Andreia reacted and began acting funnier. The audience howled! The play was a success, and Kofi and Andreia took first place in the show!

Complete a Story Map. Then answer the questions.

1. What problem do the characters face? How do they fix it?

_____

_____

_____

2. Why is the play a success? What do you think might have happened if Jin had stayed?

_____

_____

_____

Geographical Names, Historical Periods

Nouns that name a particular geographical place or period in history are proper nouns. The first letter of each important word is capitalized.

> • Examples of geographical places are mountain ranges like the Himalayas, regions like the Middle East, and sites like the Olduvai Gorge or Niagara Falls.
>
> • Some examples of historical periods are the Neolithic Age or the Baroque Period.

Thinking Question
Is the noun the name of a particular geographic place or historical period?

Write each sentence correctly.

1. Donatello was a painter during the renaissance period.

_____

2. Did you ever visit angel falls in venezuela?

_____

3. We saw pictures of the valley of kings in egypt.

_____

4. The first pyramid was built in the early dynastic period.

_____

5. The bronze age began in the near east in 3300 B.C.E.

_____

6. Paintings from the ice age were found in lascaux cave in france.

_____

Who Am I?

Read each clue. Then write the correct word on the line.

1. Every day has 24 of me. _____

2. Wolves and bears wear me. _____

3. If you fall into me you might get hurt.

   _____

4. I am all, not just part. _____

5. I am first! _____

6. My leaves are needles. _____

7. I am something people do with their ears.

   _____

8. I am something a team did. _____

Challenge   Explain the meanings of *peace* and *piece*.

_____

_____

Spelling Words

1. hole
2. whole
3. its
4. it's
5. hear
6. here
7. won
8. one
9. our
10. hour
11. their
12. there
13. fur
14. fir

Review
road
rode

Challenge
peace
piece

Idioms

Read the web below. Write the meaning of each idiom. (You may find the meanings by looking up *head* in the dictionary.)

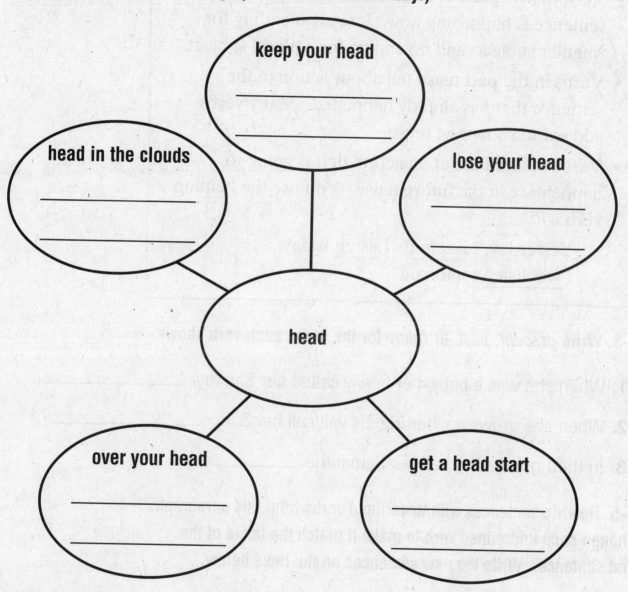

Choose one idiom from above and write two sentences. In the first sentence, write the meaning of the idiom. In the second sentence, replace the meaning with the idiom.

1. _____

2. _____

Lesson 12
PRACTICE BOOK

Simple Verb Tenses

The Science Fair
Grammar:
Spiral Review

- Verbs in the **present tense** tell that the action in the sentence is happening now. Use an -s ending for singular subjects and no ending for a plural subject.
- Verbs in the **past tense** tell about action in the sentence that has already happened. Many verbs add -ed to show past tense.
- Verbs that tell about an action that is going to happen are in the **future tense**. You use the helping verb *will*.

> Yesterday, I <u>listened</u>. I <u>listen</u> today.
> I <u>will listen</u> tomorrow.

1–3. Write *present*, *past*, or *future* for the tense each verb shows.

1. When she was a baby, her family called her Sammy. _____

2. When she grows up, her friends will call her Sam. _____

3. In third grade, they call her Samantha. _____

4–5. Rewrite sentences with underlined verbs from this paragraph. Change each underlined verb to make it match the tense of the first sentence. Write the new sentences on the lines below.

> Our dog, Yappy, ran into the street. My brother <u>calls</u> to him very loudly. Yappy <u>will stop</u> for my brother.

4. _____

5. _____

Name _____ Date _____

Proofreading for Spelling

Find the misspelled words and circle them. Then write each word correctly.

Dear Pat,

    I'm writing this in the shade of a big fur tree whose soft needles cover the ground like a blanket. Its a quiet summer day in the city's biggest park. All around, their is a feeling of piece and restfulness. My dog, Corvo, lies lazily in the hot sun. I'll bet his fir makes him hot on this summer day. I pick up a peace of paper that someone has left on the ground. Let's keep the city clean! I've been hear an our, and I could stay all day. I can hardly here the traffic. The cars with there noise seem far away. I like writing letters, but I wish you were here!

                    Your friend,

                    Chris

Spelling Words

Basic
1. hole
2. whole
3. its
4. it's
5. hear
6. here
7. won
8. one
9. our
10. hour
11. their
12. there
13. fur
14. fir

Review
road
rode

Challenge
peace
piece

1. _____   6. _____

2. _____   7. _____

3. _____   8. _____

4. _____   9. _____

5. _____   10. _____

Sentence Fluency

Using the same pronoun over and over can cause the reader to forget whom or what you are talking about. Change some pronouns to proper nouns to make your sentences clearer.

Too Many Pronouns

Ralph taught Pete many French words. He loved all the sounds he taught him.

Pronouns Changed to Proper Nouns

Ralph taught Pete many French words. Pete loved all the sounds Ralph taught him.

Replace the underlined pronouns in the paragraph with nouns that tell whom or what the sentences are talking about.

The dictionary was beside the pencil. <u>It</u> was left there. <u>It</u> will be picked up later, when students look up words. Ted needs <u>it</u> to write his homework with Leon. <u>He</u> is a very good writer. <u>He</u> needs help from Ted.

1. _____

2. _____

3. _____

4. _____

5. _____

Contractions with *n't*, *'d*, *'ve*

**Yonder Mountain:
A Cherokee Legend**

Phonics: Contractions
with *n't*, *'d*, *'ve*

**Read each sentence. Choose the missing word
from the box. Write the word. Then reread the complete sentence.**

aren't	couldn't	should've
they'd	you'd	haven't
I've	we've	I'd

1. If I ever had to sleep in the woods,

_____ bring lots of bug spray.

2. I tried to open the jar, but I _____ because
the lid was on too tight.

3. If you saw the movie, _____ love it as much
as I did.

4. My parents _____ too strict, but they do
have some rules.

5. Personally, _____ always admired Ben
Franklin.

6. You and I may not be best friends, but _____
worked out some of our differences.

7. "I _____ known that you were behind all of
this," said the hero to the villain.

8. Why are you serving us dessert when we _____
even eaten dinner yet?

9. If our friends saw us, _____ be really surprised.

Subject-Verb Agreement

- A verb that tells about an action that is happening now is in the **present tense.** Verbs in the present have two forms. The correct form to use depends on the subject of the sentence.

> **Thinking Question**
> *Is the noun in the subject singular or plural?*

- Add *-s* to the verb when the noun in the subject is singular. Do not add *-s* to the verb when the noun in the subject is plural.

> The word *Cherokee* <u>means</u> "people who live in the mountains."
>
> The Cherokees now <u>live</u> in Oklahoma and North Carolina.

Underline the correct present-tense verb in parentheses. Then write each sentence correctly.

1. People (hear, hears) the Cherokee language.

_____

2. Fur trader Abraham Wood (send, sends) two men.

_____

3. The program about the Cherokee (begins, begin) at 7:00.

_____

4. Cherokees (moves, move) to the west in the 1880s.

_____

Name _____ Date _____

Compare and Contrast

Read the selection below.

My name is Jim Rogers. I live with my parents and my brother in Oklahoma. One day last year, my brother Dennis and I were playing a board game when our father came home. He asked us to stop playing for a moment. He had some news.

Dad told us that he'd been offered a new job. The problem was that the job was in California. He wanted to know how Dennis and I felt about leaving Oklahoma.

Dennis is younger than I am, and he started to get excited. He really wanted Dad to take the offer. He dashed into his room and came back with a big book. "This book has pictures of California," he said to Dad and me. He opened the book and showed us some of them. "I think California is the greatest place on Earth," Dennis said.

I understood why my brother was excited about moving, but I felt sad at the thought. I asked Dad to go for a walk to talk about it. Dennis came too.

After the walk, Dad looked at me and Dennis. He thanked us for sharing our feelings. Then he said he thought I was right.

"Some things," he said, "are more important than money. We've got a great life here in Oklahoma. I think we will stay put."

Use a chart to compare and contrast Jim and Dennis.

Jim	Dennis

More Subject-Verb Agreement

- Some verbs end with *-es* instead of *-s*. Add *-es* to verbs that end with *s*, *sh*, *ch*, or *x* when they are used with a singular noun in the subject. Do not add *-es* when the noun in the subject is plural.
- Some verbs end with a consonant and *y*. Change the *y* to *i*, and add *-es* when you use this kind of verb with a singular noun.

    The town searches for a new music director.
    A singer worries it will not happen.

- The verb *search* adds *-es*. The verb *worry* changes the *y* to *i* and adds *-es*.

Thinking Question
*Does the verb end
in s, sh, ch, x, or with
a consonant and y?*

Underline the correct present-tense verb in parentheses. Then write each sentence correctly.

1. A newspaper writer (asks, askes) for a new music director.

   _____

2. A town citizen (watchs, watches) for a new music director.

   _____

3. A woman who knows music (hurrys, hurries) into town.

   _____

4. She (trys, tries) to get everyone to sing well together.

   _____

Name _____ Date _____

Lesson 13
PRACTICE BOOK

Yonder Mountain:
A Cherokee Legend
Spelling:
Contractions

Contractions

Write each Basic Word under the correct heading.

Contractions combining a base word and *not*	Contractions combining a base word and *is*, *us*, or *has*
_____	_____
_____	_____
_____	_____
_____	_____
_____	_____
_____	_____

Contractions combining a base word and *are*	Contractions combining a base word and *had* or *would*
_____	_____
_____	_____
_____	_____

Challenge: Add the Challenge Words to your Word Sort.

Spelling Words

Basic
1. I'd
2. he's
3. haven't
4. doesn't
5. let's
6. there's
7. wouldn't
8. what's
9. she's
10. aren't
11. hasn't
12. couldn't
13. he'd
14. they're

Review
can't
isn't

Challenge
we're
weren't

Name _____ Date _____

Lesson 13
PRACTICE BOOK

Yonder Mountain:
A Cherokee Legend
Writing:
Write to Narrate

Focus Trait: Organization
Rhyming Couplets

Rhyming couplets are two lines that have the same number of beats in each line and that end in words that rhyme. Words rhyme when the end sound of the words are the same. The words *win* and *tin* rhyme.

Fill in the blanks in the couplets below to make rhyming couplets. Use the words in the box below for ideas, or think of your own rhyming words.

Rhyming Words		
bed	where	race
bike	fun	

1. The cat jumped up into the air,

   And then it hid. I don't know _____.

2. I love my dog, and his name is Ned.

   He's black and soft and sleeps on my _____.

3. I ran and ran and kept up my pace.

   At the end of the day I had won the _____.

4. Finally, finally my homework is done.

   Now I can play and have some _____.

5. On Saturdays I always hike.

   On other days I ride my _____.

Cumulative Review

**Write a word from the box to complete each sentence.
Then read the sentence.**

road	they've	we've
you'd	I'd	rode
aren't	hasn't	didn't

1. If you _____ leave the door open, who did?

2. We were on the _____ at six in the morning.

3. This old trunk _____ been opened in years.

4. Eric and Marc have no idea how to get to the beach

because _____ never been there.

5. _____ guess that you are hungry after
working all day.

6. Carla and Shannon _____ old enough to
stay up so late.

7. Dee was excited to tell her friends how she

_____ a horse on vacation.

8. If _____ just listen more, and talk less, you
could learn a lot more.

9. My cousin pulled me outside, saying, "_____
got to leave now!"

Name _____ Date _____

Lesson 13
PRACTICE BOOK

**Yonder Mountain:
A Cherokee Legend**
Deepen Comprehension:
Compare and Contrast

Compare and Contrast

Read the selection below.

Once, many years ago, it was winter in what is now Pennsylvania. The snow fell often. The cold weather froze the rivers. Many plants, trees, and animals died.

One day, a young girl named Bright Eyes was walking along a snowy path. She'd been asked by her mother to gather firewood.

"We've got to find some more food," Bright Eyes said aloud.

Just then, Bright Eyes saw a brown rabbit, pausing in the white snow. The rabbit soon dashed away, but Bright Eyes followed the animal's tracks.

The tracks led Bright Eyes into the woods. She saw a large pile of branches and knew she could use them for firewood.

When Bright Eyes moved the branches, she was amazed by what she saw. Under the mound were hundreds of mushrooms. The branches had protected them from the snow and cold. She knew that the mushrooms would feed her family for weeks.

Bright Eyes did not pick all of the mushrooms. She left some and covered them again with the branches. They would continue to grow. She could then return for more if her family needed food later in the winter.

Compare and contrast Bright Eyes with Black Bear and Gray Wolf from "Yonder Mountain: A Cherokee Legend." Use a chart like the one shown here. Then answer the questions below.

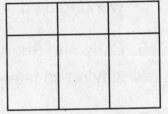

1. What words would you use to describe Bright Eyes in this story? How is what happens to Bright Eyes similar to what happens to Black Bear and Gray Wolf?

_____

_____

2. If you were Bright Eyes, would you take back all the mushrooms to your family or leave some for later? Give reasons for your answer.

_____

_____

Subject-Verb Agreement

**Yonder Mountain:
A Cherokee Legend**
Grammar:
Subject-Verb Agreement

**The subject of each sentence is underlined. Write the
correct form of the verb in parentheses to complete each sentence.**

1. A <u>climber</u> _____ for a way to the top. (search)

2. Two strong <u>men</u> _____ themselves up the cliffs. (pull)

3. A <u>woman</u> _____ her ropes to be safe. (fix)

4. One <u>person</u> _____ another as they climb. (pass)

5. <u>Friends</u> _____ someone who is tired. (help)

6. Some <u>boys</u> _____ to see who can be first to the top. (race)

7. A <u>bird</u> _____ up to the highest point. (fly)

8. One <u>group</u> _____ a deep valley on the way. (cross)

9. One tired <u>person</u> _____ on the way up. (slip)

10. A short <u>woman</u> _____ the top of the mountain first. (reach)

Contractions

Write the spelling word that is a contraction of each word pair below.

1. have not _____

2. what is _____

3. let us _____

4. he had _____

5. could not _____

6. there is _____

7. are not _____

8. she is _____

9. they are _____

10. does not _____

11. I had _____

12. would not _____

13. he is _____

14. has not _____

Spelling Words

1. I'd
2. he's
3. haven't
4. doesn't
5. let's
6. there's
7. wouldn't
8. what's
9. she's
10. aren't
11. hasn't
12. couldn't
13. he'd
14. they're

Review
can't
isn't

Challenge
we're
weren't

Lesson 13
PRACTICE BOOK

**Yonder Mountain:
A Cherokee Legend**
Vocabulary Strategies:
Homophones/Homographs

Homophones/Homographs

Read the following paragraph. Proofread it to find mistakes with homophones. Write the wrong homophone and the correct homophone on the lines.

My grandmother and I walked to the park. On our weigh, we passed a fruit stand.

"Mind if we peak at your selection?" my grandmother asked.

"Go ahead!" the fruit vendor said. "I have all kinds of fresh fruits write here! Here, have this red pare," he added. "It's perfectly ripe."

"Thanks," my grandmother said. "I almost mist that one!"

1. _____

2. _____

3. _____

4. _____

5. _____

Choose a pair of homophones. Write a sentence that shows the meaning of each word.

_____

_____

Writing Correct Sentences

- End a statement with a period, a question with a question mark, a command with a period, and an exclamation with an exclamation point.

  We're climbing now. Do you have some rope?
  Give it to me. This is so exciting!

- Two or more sentences that run together are called run-on sentences. Use end marks and capital letters correctly to keep sentences from running together.

  Help us get the rope they need it.

  Help us get the rope. They need it.

Correct each run-on sentence. Write it as two sentences.

Use correct capital letters and end marks.

1. A man named Hillary climbed the tallest mountain it is named Everest

_____

2. He climbed it in 1953 he did it with a guide

_____

3. Hillary was born in New Zealand the date was July 20, 1919.

_____

4. Edmund Hillary died in January 2008 he was 88 years old.

_____

Proofreading

Yonder Mountain:
A Cherokee Legend
Spelling:
Contractions

Circle the ten misspelled Spelling Words in the following story. Then write each word correctly.

Spelling Words

1. I'd
2. he's
3. haven't
4. doesn't
5. let's
6. there's
7. wouldn't
8. what's
9. she's
10. aren't
11. hasn't
12. couldn't
13. he'd
14. they're

Review
can't
isn't

Challenge
we're
weren't

My Relatives

My aunt and uncle are very different from a lot of people. Hes a clown in a circus, and she works as a stuntwoman. Theyr'e always doing crazy stuff. For example, my aunt has'nt cut her hair in fifteen years. I know I couln'ot go six months without getting a haircut. Then theres the house where they live. Lets' just say that it is unique. For starters, it do'snot have any corners. You wouldnt believe how odd it looks. When we stay with them, I feel like wer'e living in a donut! If they were'nt so nice, I might think that there was actually something wrong with them.

1. _____
2. _____
3. _____
4. _____
5. _____
6. _____
7. _____
8. _____
9. _____
10. _____

Conventions: Proofreading

Proofreading is important to make writing clear and correct to the reader. Pay attention to endings of verbs as you proofread.

Singular Subject	Plural Subject
The Native American chief leads.	Chiefs lead.
He mixes an herb as medicine.	They mix herbs as medicine.
The chief thinks about his people.	Chiefs think about their people.
He works for a solution.	They work for a solution.

Proofread the paragraph. Find five errors with the spelling of verbs that show the present tense. Write the corrected sentences.

The chief of the Native American group knows it is time to move. The land lack the food needed for their people. It is time to go south. The women carries the things they want to bring. Some men on horses searches for a place to stay. They find a wonderful place by the river. The children rushes to get there first. Everyone enjoys the new area. A horse splash through the river water. Everyone smiles for the first time in a long time.

1. _____

2. _____

3. _____

4. _____

5. _____

Words with *ar, or, ore*

Read each sentence. Choose the missing word from the box.
Write the word. Then reread the sentence.

Mars	morning	cart
chores	parking	largest
artistic	explore	parlor

1. My house is the _____ house on the street.

2. "Step into my _____," said the spider to
the fly.

3. The bold scientists planned to _____ the
bottom of the ocean.

4. The driver looked for a _____ space for five
minutes.

5. Put your groceries in the _____.

6. _____ is my favorite time of day.

7. Painting, singing, and dancing are _____
hobbies.

8. I wish I could fly to the planet _____.

9. Taking out the trash and making my bed are on my list of

_____.

Name _____ Date _____

Pronoun-Verb Agreement

- Verbs show action in sentences and when that action happens. Verbs that tell about actions that are happening now are in the **present tense**.
- You add -*s* or -*es* to the verb when the pronoun in the subject is *he*, *she*, or *it*.
- You do not add -*s* or -*es* to the verb when the pronoun in the subject is *I*, *you*, *we*, or *they*.

  She <u>barks</u> very loudly.

  They <u>bark</u> even more loudly.

Thinking Question
Does the subject pronoun refer just to one person or does it refer either to me or to more than one person?

Underline the correct present-tense verb in parentheses. Then write each sentence correctly.

1. You (find, finds) dogs of all different types.

   _____

2. He (choose, chooses) the ones that are the best.

   _____

3. It (seem, seems) that you know dogs well.

   _____

4. We (feel, feels) that you should choose the dogs.

   _____

5. They (want, wants) to pick out some dogs, too.

   _____

Author's Purpose

Read the passage below.

The first animals that human beings tamed were dogs. The earliest dogs probably came from wolves or related animals. Perhaps people found wolf cubs and raised them. The cubs quickly learned how to live with people. The oldest dog bones that scientists have found are about 12,000 years old.

The next animals to be tamed were sheep, goats, cattle, and pigs. People used them for meat, dairy, and wool. These four types of farm animals were first tamed about 11,000 to 9,000 years ago.

House cats were first bred more than 5,000 years ago. People also began to tame horses about 5,000 years ago in central Asia. They were first used for milk and meat. Later, people began to ride them.

People later learned to tame other kinds of animals, including camels, chickens, and elephants. You'll never guess what the most recent animal to be tamed is. It's the hamster! All hamsters were wild until 1930. That year, someone captured a wild female hamster and her young. Scientists used the hamsters in experiments. Today, every single pet hamster comes from that first captured mother and her babies!

Complete the Inference Map to show details in the selection that help you infer the author's purpose. Write complete sentences.

Text Detail	Text Detail	Text Detail

Purpose

More Pronoun-Verb Agreement

- Most verbs in the present end with -*s* when the pronoun in the subject is *he*, *she*, or *it*. Add -*es* to verbs that end in -*s*, -*sh*, -*ch*, or -*x*.

- Do not add -*s* or -*es* to verbs when the pronoun in the subject is *I*, *you*, *we*, or *they*.

- Some verbs end with a consonant and *y*. Change the *y* to *i* and add -*es* when the pronoun in the subject is *he, she,* or *it*.

- You do not change the *y* to *i* and add -*es* when the pronoun in the subject is *I, you, we,* or *they*.

Thinking Question
Does the verb end in s, sh, ch, x or with a consonant and y, and what is the pronoun in the subject?

Underline the correct present-tense verb in parentheses. Then write each sentence correctly.

1. You (push, pushes) the cart filled with hay out to the fields.

_____

2. It (pass, passes) over the old bridge.

_____

3. We (guess, guesses) when you will reach the horses.

_____

4. They (march, marches) across the hills to the food.

_____

Words with Vowel + /r/ Sounds

Write the correct Basic Words in each box.

Write the words that contain the vowel + r sound in *far*.	Write the words that contain the vowel + r sound in *or*.
_____	_____
_____	_____
_____	_____
_____	_____
	_____
	_____
	_____

Spelling Words

Basic
1. horse
2. mark
3. storm
4. market
5. acorn
6. artist
7. March
8. north
9. barking
10. stork
11. thorn
12. forest
13. chore
14. restore

Review
dark
story

Challenge
partner
fortune

Challenge

1. Does *partner* contain the vowel sound in *far* or the vowel sound in *or*? _____

2. Does *fortune* contain the vowel sound in *far* or the vowel sound in *or*? _____

Name _____ Date _____

Lesson 14
PRACTICE BOOK

Aero and Officer Mike
Writing:
Write to Narrate

Focus Trait: Ideas
Choosing an Important Event and Purpose

An autobiography tells the story, or part of the story, of a person's life. Good autobiographers ask, *What experiences have I had that my readers would like to know about?*

Look carefully at the chart below. Look at the events and the author's purpose. Circle the event that you think readers will find most interesting and best fits the author's purpose. On the lines provided below the chart, give reasons for your answer.

Events	Author's Purpose
getting lost at the mall, learning to ride a bike, spending time with my grandmother, visiting the Grand Canyon	To tell readers about an important lesson I learned

_____

_____

_____

Name _____ Date _____

Lesson 14
PRACTICE BOOK

Cumulative Review

Write words from the box to complete the lines of the poem.

arm	garden	I'd	shark	storm
bored	harm	I've	shore	thorns

What Didn't Go Wrong Today?

I worked in my_____, but I soon came to _____.
　　　　　　　　　　 1　　　　　　　　　　　　　　　　　　　　 2

The sharp _____ of a rose badly scratched up
　　　　　　　　 3

my _____!
　　　　 4

So I went to the _____, for a swim and some sun,
　　　　　　　　　　　 5

Until a _____ showed its fin and scared everyone!
　　　　　　 6

Then _____ just reached the woods, the shade of tall trees,
　　　　　 7

When a dark _____ filled the sky and rained on the seas!
　　　　　　　 8

Now, _____ come home, sad, with nothing to do.
　　　　 9

If you are _____, too, may I come play with you?
　　　　　　　 10

Author's Purpose

Read the selection.

When a puppy is born, it has many things to learn. Its owners have things to learn too, especially if they have not had a dog before. For example, a new owner may not know how much to feed the puppy. A puppy should be fed three or more times a day for its first ten or twelve weeks. A young puppy should only eat dog food. After the puppy is about ten weeks old, it can be fed twice a day.

Early in the puppy's life, other things are happening too. After the puppy is five weeks old, the owner can begin to train the pup. The owner teaches the pup how to obey and how to behave on walks.

Then there are the puppy's shots. Pups usually get their rabies shots when they are about four months old. Until a puppy is four or five months old, it should not go near sick dogs or stray dogs.

Once it has been properly trained, the growing puppy is ready to take its place in the family. A well-trained dog is happy to be with people, and it knows what its owners expect.

Use an Inference Map to help you determine the author's purpose. Then answer the questions below.

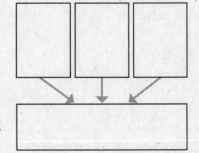

1. Why do you think the author wrote this text?

_____

_____

2. What is the author's message about puppies and dogs?
Use details from the selection to support your answer.

_____

_____

_____

Pronoun-Verb Agreement

Write the correct present-tense form of the verb in parentheses to complete each sentence.

1. I _____ with my cats to train them. (sleep)

2. They _____ my smell and trust me. (learn)

3. He _____ other ways to get close to his cats. (use)

4. She _____ them right out of her hand. (feed)

5. You _____ here and watch us do it. (sit)

6. We _____ water into their faces to test them. (splash)

7. It _____ your attention when you see it. (catch)

8. He _____ a special blend of pet food. (mix)

9. She _____ other food out in the yard. (bury)

10. They _____ the different ways to train pets. (study)

Words with Vowel + /r/ Sounds

Write eight words that are names for people, places, or things.

_____

_____

_____

_____

_____

_____

_____

_____

Challenge

1. A person you work with is your _____.

2. If you make a lot of money, you make a

_____.

Spelling Words

1. horse
2. mark
3. storm
4. market
5. acorn
6. artist
7. March
8. north
9. barking
10. stork
11. thorn
12. forest
13. chore
14. restore

Review
dark
story

Challenge
partner
fortune

Prefixes *in-, im-*

Read each base word. Add the prefix shown and write
a new word and its meaning.

Base Word	Prefix	New Word	Meaning
active	in		
visible	in		
definite	in		
patient	im		
perfect	im		
measurable	im		

Now write a sentence for each word above with a prefix. Make
sure your sentence shows the word's meaning.

1. _____

2. _____

3. _____

4. _____

5. _____

6. _____

Simple Subjects and Simple Predicates

> * The **subject** of a sentence tells whom or what the sentence is about. The main word in the subject is often a **noun**. It is called the **simple subject**.
> * The **predicate** of a sentence tells what the subject is, was, or will be, or what the subject is, was, or will be doing. The main word in the predicate is a **verb**. It is called the **simple predicate**.
>
> The <u>sheep</u> <u>ate</u> grass in the valley.
> An old <u>wolf</u> <u>watched</u> them from the bushes.

1–4. The subject of each sentence is underlined. Write the noun in the subject.

1. <u>The old gray coyote</u> came out of the hills. _____

2. <u>This smart animal</u> will eat almost anything. _____

3. <u>His little pups</u> hide right behind him. _____

4. <u>These sweet babies</u> are hungry and tired. _____

5–8. The predicate of each sentence is underlined. Write the verb in the predicate.

5. Three fat sheep <u>walk away from the others.</u> _____

6. A big blue truck <u>drives by them.</u> _____

7. A man with boots <u>grabs the sheep.</u> _____

8. The coyote <u>finds food for the pups.</u> _____

Words with Vowel + /r/ Sounds

Aero and Officer Mike
Spelling:
Vowel + /r/ Sounds

Find the misspelled words and circle them. Then write each word correctly.

An ortist was traveling through a deep, dark farest. He carried his paints and brushes in a bag that hung from his back. His harse was white, just like a blank canvas. He was riding to the morket, a day's ride to the narth, to sell his pictures. Suddenly, huge gray clouds moved overhead. A starm was coming! The wind rose, and an acarn fell from a tree, hitting the man on the head. A sharp tharn from a bush stung his hand. A big white stark flapped its wings as it flew toward its nest. Then the traveler heard the borking of wild dogs in the distance. "Don't worry," he told his horse. "They're afraid of thunder and lightning."

Spelling Words

1. horse
2. mark
3. storm
4. market
5. acorn
6. artist
7. March
8. north
9. barking
10. stork
11. thorn
12. forest
13. chore
14. restore

Review
dark
story

Challenge
partner
fortune

1. _____   6. _____

2. _____   7. _____

3. _____   8. _____

4. _____   9. _____

5. _____   10. _____

Sentence Fluency

Combining two sentences that have the same noun in the subject makes your writing smoother and easier to read. Remember to use a comma and the word *and*.

Same Noun in the Subject	Pronoun Replacing Noun in the Subject
These dogs are for sports. These dogs make great pets.	These dogs are for sports, and they make great pets.
Border collies are herding dogs. Border collies are very smart.	Border collies are herding dogs, and they are very smart.

Combine each pair of sentences. Change each underlined subject to a pronoun. Write the new sentence.

1. Maltese dogs are friendly. <u>Maltese dogs</u> make good pets.

_____

2. My male Great Dane is very gentle. <u>My male Great Dane</u> stands very tall.

_____

3. Your female collie tends sheep. <u>Your female collie</u> gets burrs in her fur.

_____

4. The people who breed dogs work very hard. <u>The people who breed dogs</u> love animals.

_____

5. My family and I look for the perfect dog. <u>My family and I</u> find a funny one we love.

_____

Words with *er, ir, ur, or*

**Read each sentence. Choose the missing word from the box.
Write the word. Then reread the complete sentence.**

curb	nerve	curves
worker	furry	birth
thirty	germs	

1. The road _____ up ahead, so be ready to turn.

2. Having hair on the furniture is one of the problems with having a

   _____ dog.

3. I knew you wouldn't have the _____ to stand up to your
   big brother.

4. As Danielle crossed the street, she tripped on the _____ and
   hurt her ankle.

5. Adam does well in school because he is a hard _____.

6. Mrs. Fort gave _____ to a baby girl named Donna last week.

7. Ted decided that he wanted to own a mansion by the time he turned

   _____.

8. Colds and the flu are caused by _____.

Name _____ Date _____

Forming the Past Tense

- Most verbs show past tense by adding -ed.
- Some verbs end with e. Drop the e and add -ed.

  They <u>allowed</u> us to cook alone.

  He <u>needed</u> eggs for the recipe.

  Evan's parents <u>liked</u> our cooking.

Thinking Question
Can I add -ed to the verb to show past tense? Does the verb end in e?

Write each sentence using the correct past tense of the verb in parentheses.

1. Evan _____ his parents to send him to cooking school. (want)

   _____

2. We _____ to answer a newspaper ad for a school. (decide)

   _____

3. Many cooking students _____ there. (work)

   _____

4. Evan and I _____ that they would like our letter. (hope)

   _____

5. We _____ the school with the good work we did. (surprise)

   _____

Name _____ Date _____

Lesson 15
PRACTICE BOOK

Understanding Characters

Read the passage and look for text evidence about Brooke's character traits. Then complete the Inference Map.

Brooke and Sean wanted to do something special for Mom on Mother's Day. Brooke got out a pencil and pad and wrote down ideas about what they could do. She said, "Mom drinks tea every morning with toast. Maybe we can make her tea and toast and bring it to her in bed!"

Sean nodded, and they went into the kitchen. Brooke grabbed tea bags from the cabinet. She also took out bread and some butter. Sean filled the kettle and found the milk and sugar. Brooke neatly laid each item out on the counter. "You handle the tea, Sean," Brooke told her brother, "and I'll take care of the toast."

In a few minutes, it was ready. Brooke placed everything on a tray. They went up to Mom's bedroom. "What a great gift!" Mom exclaimed.

Mom took a bite of toast and a sip of tea. Right away, Brooke noticed something odd in Mom's expression. "This is very nice of you both," Mom said. "However, are you sure you put the tea bag in the water?"

Sean's face went white. He had served Mom hot water with milk and sugar and forgotten to add the tea!

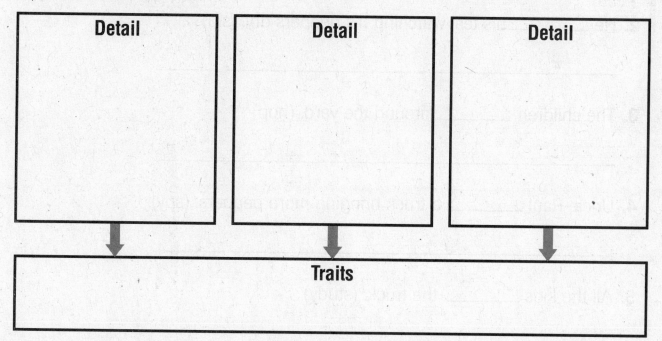

Name _____ Date _____

Forming the Past Tense

- Some verbs end with a consonant and *y*. To form the past-tense verb, change the *y* to *i*, and add *-ed*.

- Some verbs end with one vowel followed by one consonant. To form the past-tense verb, double the consonant, and add *-ed*.

- The verb *dry* ends in *y*. Change the *y* to *i*, and add *-ed*. The verb *beg* ends with one vowel followed by one consonant. Double the consonant, and add *-ed*.

> **Thinking Question**
> *Does the verb end with a consonant and y or one vowel followed by a consonant?*

Write each sentence, using the correct past-tense form of the verb in parentheses.

1. Uncle Raul _____ the drying mat. (try)

   _____

2. He _____ his tea, watching his peppers dry. (sip)

   _____

3. The children _____ around the yard. (hop)

   _____

4. Uncle Raul _____ a truck bringing more peppers. (spy)

   _____

5. All the kids _____ the truck. (study)

   _____

Vowel + /r/ Sounds in *nurse*

Write each Basic Word under the correct heading.

Words with the vowel + /r/ sound in *nurse* spelled *ur*	Words with the vowel + /r/ sound in *nurse* spelled *ir*
_____	_____
_____	_____
_____	_____
_____	_____
_____	_____

Words with the vowel + /r/ sound in *nurse* spelled *or*	Words with the vowel + /r/ sound in *nurse* spelled *er*
_____	_____
_____	_____
_____	_____

Spelling Words

Basic

1. nurse
2. work
3. shirt
4. hurt
5. first
6. word
7. serve
8. curly
9. dirt
10. third
11. worry
12. turn
13. stir
14. firm

Review
her
girl

Challenge
perfect
hamburger

Challenge: Which Challenge Word can only be placed in the last box? _____

Which Challenge Word can be placed in either the first or the last box? _____

Focus Trait: Voice
Using Details to Show Thoughts and Feelings

> Part of writing with voice means using sensory words and details that let your readers know how you feel about your topic. Compare the sentences below.

Weak Voice	Strong Voice
We saw the Grand Canyon. It was big and pretty. I had a good time.	When I first saw the Grand Canyon I couldn't believe my eyes. It was huge, scary, and incredibly beautiful. It was the very best vacation of my life!

The sentences below are weak in voice. Rewrite them adding details that show thoughts and feelings.

1. It was stormy. I heard wind.

   _____

   _____

2. It was a nice day. We went hiking.

   _____

   _____

3. The swing broke.

   _____

   _____

4. She called my name.

   _____

Name _____ Date _____

Cumulative Review

Write a word from the box to complete each sentence. Then read
the sentence.

certainly	herd	working
firmly	turning	burger
spark	report	before

1. This restaurant is known for having a great

   _____ and tasty fries.

2. This vacation is _____ into a bad trip now
   that we're lost and out of money.

3. Damon gave a very interesting _____ about
   the rain forests.

4. I _____ don't want to spend all weekend
   studying.

5. The forest fire began with just a single _____.

6. Nicole was being silly when she said that she always ate

   lunch _____ breakfast.

7. Frank held the ball _____ as he ran.

8. The cowboys rounded up the _____ of
   cattle.

9. Because the dryer is not _____, my clothes
   are still wet.

Understanding Characters

Read the selection.

Mom was in the kitchen making apple pie. She called me in to help her. I was shocked. This was the first time she had ever let anyone help her. No one even knew Mom's recipe! Mom started to make the pie crust. Then she handed me an apple. "Peel this," Mom said.

I began peeling the apple with great care. Right away, I noticed the apple smelled rotten. I grabbed another and started peeling. It was rotten, too. "Mom," I began, "I think these apples are rotten."

Mom stopped and turned. She sliced open another apple, and another. They were all rotten. Mom said, "I guess we'll have to try something new."

Within moments, Mom had a bag of potatoes in front of me. Mom just substituted potatoes for apples in her recipe!

So how did the apple-less pie taste? Honestly, it was delicious, and she gave me credit for helping her to invent it!

Use an Inference Map to write about Mom's traits. Use it to help you answer the questions below.

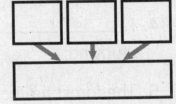

1. The narrator says that she is "shocked" when Mom asks for her help. Based on what you know about Mom, does this reaction seem realistic? Explain.

   _____

   _____

   _____

2. Based on what Mom says, does, and thinks in this story, predict how she would react if there had not been any potatoes in the house.

   _____

   _____

   _____

Forming the Past Tense

1–4. Write each sentence using the correct past-tense form of the verb in parentheses.

1. Theo _____ to study recipes. (love)

_____

2. He _____ them over and over again. (turn)

_____

3. We _____ through recipes looking for a perfect meal. (race)

_____

4. We _____ it when we found one. (like)

_____

5–8. Write the correct past-tense form of the verb in parentheses. The underlined letters are spelling clues.

5. The pan _____ the chicken. (fr<u>y</u>)

6. One of us _____ to take it out before it was done. (tr<u>y</u>)

7. The younger kids _____ how I did it. (stud<u>y</u>)

8. Two of us _____ dishes to the table. (carry)

Vowel + /r/ Sounds in *nurse*

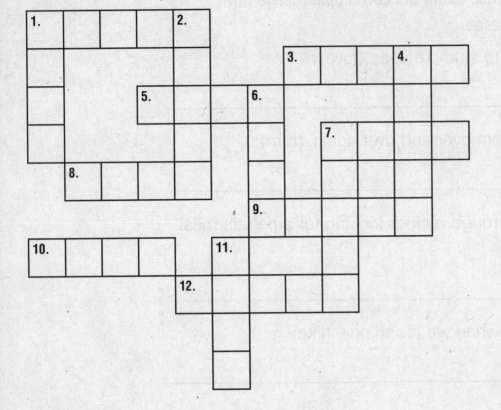

Spelling Words

1. nurse
2. work
3. shirt
4. hurt
5. first
6. word
7. serve
8. curly
9. dirt
10. third
11. worry
12. turn
13. stir
14. firm

Review
her
girl

Challenge
perfect
hamburger

Use the Basic Words to complete the puzzle.

Across

1. Item of clothing
3. Comes before "second"
5. Soil
7. The opposite of play
8. "Please" is the magic _____.
9. A hospital worker
10. Not soft
12. The opposite of straight

Down

1. To mix
2. Comes after "second"
4. To present or give
6. Move a car right or left
7. Be concerned
11. Injured

Name _____ Date _____

Lesson 15
PRACTICE BOOK

The Extra-good Sunday
Vocabulary Strategies:
Using a Thesaurus

Using a Thesaurus

Read the book review. Look up each underlined word in a
thesaurus. Write a synonym for each word.

> If you haven't already, you'll want to meet Ramona Quimby. The
> latest adventures of this special girl appear in *Ramona Quimby, Age 8*.
> With her father in college and her mother back at work, Ramona has
> to resolve some things for herself. How will she handle her annoying
> young neighbor? Will her parents be cross with her when she makes a
> mess? Will things remain tense with Yard Ape?
>
> There is a reason why Beverly Cleary's books remain some of
> America's favorites after so many years.

1. _____

2. _____

3. _____

4. _____

5. _____

6. _____

Write two sentences that could be in your own review of *The
Extra-good Sunday*. Choose a word in each sentence to look up in
a thesaurus. Write a synonym for each word.

7. _____

8. _____

Kinds of Pronouns

- A pronoun is a word that can take the place of one or more nouns in a sentence. The pronouns *I*, *you*, *he*, *she*, *it*, *we*, and *they* are subject pronouns. Pronouns can be singular or plural.
- The words *me*, *you*, *him*, *her*, *it*, *us*, and *them* are called object pronouns. Object pronouns follow action verbs and words like *to*, *for*, *at*, *of*, and *with*.

     Claude did not understand his **parents**.

     He did not understand **them**.

1–2. Write each sentence. Replace the underlined word or words with a subject or object pronoun.

1. <u>Claude</u> thinks his parents are good people.

   _____

2. Claude shows respect to <u>his parents</u>.

   _____

3–4. Replace the repeated noun in these sentences with a pronoun. Write the new sentences on the line.

3. Claude loves to eat. Claude enjoys eating with his family.

   _____

4. Claude loves his friends. His friends see him every day.

   _____

Name _____ Date _____

Proofread for Spelling

The Extra-good Sunday
Spelling:
Vowel + /r/ Sounds in *nurse*

Circle the ten misspelled Spelling Words in this diary entry.
Then write each word correctly.

June 2nd

Today was the purfect day. Dad decided
to take a day off from wirk, and we went to the
baseball game. Our seats were on the ferst base
side of the field. The grass looked so green, and
the durt on the infield looked so soft. As we
sat down, Dad smiled and asked if my hair was
getting more cirly. Before I could say a wurd, I
saw my favorite player. He is the therd baseman,
and he wears number 20 on his shurt. That's my
favorite number, too! The last time we came to
a game, he was hirt, but he was healthy today.
Dad ordered me a hambirgur, and we settled in to
watch a great game.

Spelling Words
1. nurse
2. work
3. shirt
4. hurt
5. first
6. word
7. serve
8. curly
9. dirt
10. third
11. worry
12. turn
13. stir
14. firm

Review
her
girl

Challenge
perfect
hamburger

1. _____ 6. _____
2. _____ 7. _____
3. _____ 8. _____
4. _____ 9. _____
5. _____ 10. _____

Word Choice

Using exact verbs helps the reader better picture what you are saying or writing about.

Less Exact Verb	More Exact Verb
made	cooked, roasted
put	arranged, scooped
touched	patted
moved	danced, flipped
grew	expanded

Replace each underlined verb in the sentences with a more exact verb. Use the verbs in the word box.

1. The family <u>made</u> dinner all together. _____

2. Sister Kate <u>made</u> their favorite meat in the oven. _____

3. The younger kids <u>put</u> plates and glasses on the table. _____

4. Brother Lance <u>put</u> ice cream into dishes. _____

5. Dad <u>touched</u> the rolls to make them flat. _____

6. Harry <u>moved</u> pancakes in the pan. _____

7. The people <u>moved</u> around the table. _____

8. The bread <u>grew</u> in the oven. _____